SCHOLAS

MW00813683

The Fluent Reader *in ACTION*

A **Close-Up** Look Into
15 Diverse Classrooms

Timothy V. Rasinski
Robert Ackland
Gay Fawcett
Kristin Lems

New York • Toronto • London • Auckland • Sydney
Mexico City • New Delhi • Hong Kong • Buenos Aires

Teaching *Resources*

We dedicate this book to the wonderful teachers of reading fluency featured in this book who so graciously allowed us to enter their classrooms and tell their stories of developing proficient readers through effective and creative approaches to fluency instruction. We especially want to remember Susie Greathouse, one of the teachers in the book, who recently passed away. While telling her story painfully reminds us of the loss, we are happy that the influence she had on thousands of children, parents, and colleagues will live on, and increase, through the story she shared for this book.

Cover design: Emil Meek
Interior design: Holly Grundon

ISBN: 978-0-439-63340-6

Copyright © 2011 by Timothy V. Rasinski, Robert Ackland, Gay Fawcett, and Kristin Lems

All rights reserved. Published by Scholastic Inc.
Printed in the U.S.A.

1 2 3 4 5 6 7 8 9 10   40   17 16 15 14 13 12 11

TABLE *of Contents*

Introduction

Fluency as a concept first came on the contemporary literacy landscape in the late 1970s and early 1980s with the seminal work of Jay Samuels (1997), Carol Chomsky (1976), Peter Schreiber (1980), LaBerge and Samuels (1974), and Richard Allington (1983), among others, who argued that there is a link between automatic word recognition and text phrasing and overall reading comprehension. Not only is it important for readers to read words accurately, but they also need to read the words in text effortlessly, so that they can use their limited amount of cognitive attention to figure out meaning instead of devoting it to reading the words correctly. It is also important for readers to read words with appropriate expression (what linguists call "prosody"), so that they are able to chunk text into meaningful phrases and add meaning through vocal emphasis, volume, speed, and pausing. These early fluency scholars told us that fluency may be the missing link in effective literacy instruction.

Despite this early interest, reading fluency seemed to fly under the radar for the next two decades. Most literacy scholars continued to focus their attention on comprehension and comprehension instruction. Many teachers asked, "Why is it important to teach children to read orally and with expression? I'm interested in improving silent reading comprehension."

Finally, with the publication of the report of the National Reading Panel (NICHD, 2000a, 2000b), fluency has achieved prominence as one of the pillars of effective reading instruction. The panel summarized empirical research related to reading fluency and its instruction and concluded that fluency is an important part of effective reading instruction and that it improves in students' oral and silent reading comprehension and overall achievement in reading.

Since the panel's report, research continues to demonstrate that fluency is important at the early grade levels and beyond. For many students who experience difficulty in reading comprehension and achievement, a lack of fluency may be the culprit.

Several fine books on reading fluency have been embraced by literacy scholars, researchers, and teachers. These books provide a great introduction to fluency: defining the concept and its various components, identifying how reading fluency can be assessed and how progress in fluency can be measured, and sharing basic approaches for teaching fluency in the classroom or reading clinic.

Still, beyond the growing research and scholarly writing that supports fluency, actual models of effective and engaging fluency instruction from real classrooms are scarce. Moreover, it is generally assumed that reading fluency is an issue only for the primary grades. Beyond grades 2 or 3, it has often been thought, fluency does not need to be directly addressed in literacy instruction. Our own research, however, has discovered that fluency is an important instructional issue well beyond the primary grades, even into high school. We have found that in the intermediate and secondary grades, fluency is strongly related to overall achievement in reading and that significant numbers of students at all of these levels have not achieved sufficient fluency to comprehend well in grade-level reading tasks. It is not difficult to come to the conclusion that perhaps one of the main causes of reading difficulties beyond the primary grades is a lack of reading fluency and a lack of appropriate fluency instruction at these same grade levels.

As the literacy field begins to acknowledge that fluency is an issue beyond the primary grades, teachers and students will need engaging, workable models of authentic instruction in fluency from real classrooms and real students. The purpose of this book, then, is to fill in this gap—to provide teachers with detailed models of effective ways in which fluency is taught by teachers around the United States and in other English-speaking countries. Whether these models are used by in-service teachers on their own, in small professional development groups, or by pre-service teachers as coursework, we hope this book will provide opportunities for teachers to see fluency instruction in action, understand how fluency fits into the larger realm of school literacy instruction, think deeply about their own approaches to instruction and assessment, and make and implement their own plans for effective fluency instruction.

Defining Fluency

Just what is reading fluency? Some mistakenly believe fluency is nothing more than reading quickly. We take a much deeper view. We see fluency as the ability of readers to master the actual printed text that they see—the "surface level"—so that they may reach the "deep level," gaining meaning, or comprehending the text. Although achieving the deep level is the essential goal of reading, gaining mastery of the surface level is necessary for readers to be able to dive deep into meaning. Many readers fail to understand what they read not because they can't make sense of the text (they understand just fine if the text is read to them) but because they have not yet mastered the various tasks required at the surface level. They may not be decoding the words with sufficient accuracy; they may not be decoding the words in text with sufficient automaticity; they may not be grouping the individual words in the passage into meaningful phrases; or they may not be reading the passage with meaning-enhancing expression, or prosody. Noted literacy scholars Nell Duke, Michael Pressley, and Katherine Hilden (2004) suggest that a major cause of comprehension difficulties among a strong majority of students with significant reading difficulties is a lack of fluency, or difficulty in dealing with the surface level of texts. So, although fluency itself may not appear to concern itself directly with meaning, readers need to have fluency in place to comprehend what they read. Let's take a closer look at each of the three main components of fluency: decoding accuracy, decoding automaticity, and prosodic reading.

Word Decoding Accuracy

Accuracy in word decoding simply refers to what some scholars call the "phonics" component of reading. If students can translate or sound out the written words in text into their oral forms, they have accurate word recognition. Word decoding accuracy is the foundational component of fluency. Clearly, readers cannot read if they are unable to decode the words they encounter in print.

Although we would like to think that all students have mastered phonics and word decoding in the primary grades, the fact of the matter is that, due to the complex nature of the English orthographic system, many students still struggle with word decoding, and as a result, also struggle with comprehending what they read. Even in the upper-elementary grades, middle grades, and high school years, we need to be able to provide assistance and instruction to students in how to decode words.

Moreover, we need to provide instruction in word meaning, or vocabulary. In these grades, students begin more intense study of the various content areas and the academic words that are essential to learning in those areas. Even if students can decode those words successfully, if they do not know the meanings of the words, they will have much difficulty in achieving reading comprehension. Clearly, word study, in the form of both word decoding and vocabulary learning, needs to be incorporated into instruction for upper elementary, middle grade, and high school readers.

Automaticity in Word Decoding

Learning to decode words accurately is an essential part of fluency; however, it alone is not sufficient for a reader to be considered fluent. Automaticity is a second component of fluency. The automaticity theory of reading proposed by LaBerge and Samuels (1974) suggests that all readers have a limited amount of cognitive attention and that the attention used for one task is not available for use on another task. Have you had the experience of trying to do two or more tasks that required your attention at the same time? Chances are that you messed up, or did not do as well as you would have liked, on at least one of those tasks because you were not able to give your full attention to the task. The high number of auto accidents by drivers using their cell phones is only one dramatic example of this!

Reading requires at least two important tasks to be done simultaneously. The first is to decode the written words. The second, more important task is to comprehend or make sense of what the author is trying to convey. If readers have to devote too many of their attentional resources to the first task (word decoding), they may not have sufficient attention to perform the second (make meaning). A key to successful reading is to devote a minimal amount of attention to the first task in order to have a sufficient amount for the more important, second task. The way to minimize the first task is to make it an automatic process, something that is done effortlessly. Perhaps the best example of automatic word decoding is you—the person reading this text. Our guess is that as you read this text you are putting very little effort into decoding the words; you are not consciously using your phonics knowledge. Most of the words you encounter are processed as sight words, instantly and effortlessly recognized. The result of your automaticity in word decoding is that you can give most of your attention to making meaning out of this passage.

Automaticity in word decoding also needs to be part of effective reading fluency instruction. Automaticity can be developed through repeated practice in identifying words, particularly repeated practice of words in connected written discourse or in authentic reading—reading for real and meaningful purposes. In many classrooms today, automaticity is erroneously taught by focusing students' attention on reading faster.

Expressive, Prosodic Reading

When we think of a fluent speaker, it brings to mind someone who speaks with good expression, using the voice in concert with the words to create effective communication. When they read orally, fluent readers read in the same way, with expression in their voice. In doing so, they are able to demonstrate that they are making meaning, or monitoring and enhancing their comprehension of their reading.

Even when readers read silently, they hear their inner voice; brain research on language confirms that hearing oneself produce sounds is very important (Zadina, 2010). Thus, expressive, prosodic reading applies to silent as well as oral reading. Research has found that readers who read orally with good expression are more likely to read with higher levels of comprehension when they read silently, and readers who read with lower levels of appropriate expression and prosody are more likely to read silently with lower levels of comprehension and overall reading proficiency (Daane, Campbell, Grigg, Goodman & Oranje, 2005; Pinnell et al., 1995; Rasinski, Rikli & Johnston, 2009).

When teachers work with students to help them learn to read with good expression, to hear that "expressive voice" even when reading silently, they are asking their students to read with fluency and comprehension. Effective reading fluency instruction, then, needs to include a focus on having students read with appropriate phrasing and expression, or prosody. Prosodic reading is best taught by modeling it for students; talking with them about how their voice is able to express meaning; allowing students opportunities to practice prosodic reading so they can develop the appropriate level of expression for reading a particular text; and giving them opportunities to perform their reading for an audience that can listen and respond meaningfully.

Why This Book

All three components of reading fluency—decoding accuracy, decoding automaticity, and prosodic reading—are important and need to be part of effective reading instruction. Knowing what to teach, however, is much different than knowing *how* to teach it. It is this second part—how to teach fluency—that is the focus of this book.

We developed this book to provide you, the teacher in grade 5 or above, the opportunity to visit with upper elementary, middle school, and high school teachers we have found in varied locations who are teaching reading fluency effectively and in ways that students and teachers find engaging and enjoyable. Moreover, you will find that all the teachers we feature in this book—and its companion, *The Fluent Reader in Action: Grades PreK–4* —teach the basic components of fluency mentioned previously, but they all teach them differently.

The idea we wish to convey is that teachers make the difference. Although we know what we need to teach for fluency, how that teaching is done depends on the teacher. There is no one program or approach that works best. There are some basic principles for teaching fluency, but how those principles are actually developed and applied in real classrooms is the job of the individual teacher. We want you to see how different teachers in different teaching settings, working with different children, have developed their own approaches to teaching fluency effectively.

How to Use This Book

This book may be used individually or in small groups, read in one sitting or over the course of several days, read straight through or chapter by chapter, with opportunities for personal and group response. We recommend that the book be read, as a type of book study with other teachers over the course of several weeks. Perhaps the literacy coach in your school can act as the discussion leader.

Before reading beyond this introductory chapter, we suggest that you think about your own approach to reading fluency. In a personal notebook that would accompany your reading of this book, you may want to respond to the following questions:

* How do you define reading fluency? What does reading fluency mean to you?

* Do you consider yourself a fluent reader? Why?

* If you are a fluent reader, how did you become one?

* Rate your own knowledge of reading fluency—high, middling, low. How did you learn about reading fluency?

* What experiences have convinced you that fluency is important enough to be taught beyond the primary grades?

* How do you teach reading fluency?

* How much time do you allot for it on a daily or weekly basis?

* What constitutes fluency instruction in your classroom? What do you do, and what do you ask your students to do, in the name of fluency instruction?

* What sorts of texts do you use to teach and nurture fluency in your students?

* How do you connect fluency instruction with reading comprehension?

* How do you help students make the connection between fluency and overall proficient reading?

* What special circumstances must teachers in the upper-elementary grades and beyond need to be aware of in order to make fluency instruction work for their students?

* What thoughts or insights do you have when thinking about the connection between oral and silent reading fluency?

* How do you assess and monitor students' progress in reading fluency?

* How do you communicate the value of fluency instruction to parents and caregivers of older children?

Share your responses with others in your group. Do they have similar feelings about and experiences with fluency? Try to brainstorm as a group at least five essential questions about reading fluency that you would like to address as you engage in reading this book. Once you've done this, you are ready to dive into the chapter stories of the featured teachers.

Each chapter tells the story of a teacher who teaches one or more aspects of reading fluency in a way that, although based on the principles in this book—set forth on the following pages, is all her or his own. Please read each teacher's story, observe how challenges were overcome, and think of other dimensions that remain to be addressed, especially if you have already implemented a similar model in your own instructional setting. Examine the documents and materials that are presented in each chapter. Can you adapt them to your own teaching? Think about the teacher's evidence of success. Do you find it compelling? What else might need to be assessed if you attempted this model of instruction? Finally, how can you adapt this model—not simply transfer it—to your own instructional setting? How can you employ the model described in each chapter to fit your own personal style of teaching and the kinds of students with whom you work?

Once you have thoroughly digested a chapter, meet with your colleagues who are also using this book, and share the thoughts, concerns, and insights that you took from each chapter. What kinds of approaches or adaptations have your colleagues expressed about the models of fluency instruction? How do their responses change your own thinking?

Principles
for *Teaching Fluency*

Word study. Help students develop masterful accuracy in their word recognition/decoding/spelling, including the knowledge of the meaning of words.

Modeling fluent reading. Read to students regularly and discuss with them how you are able to make and add to meaning with various elements of your voice (such as intonation, etc.).

Supported reading. Provide fluent reading support (scaffolding) for students by allowing them to read while hearing the same text read fluently along with them.

Repeated reading. Provide opportunities for students to read particular texts several times, with the focus being reading with expression. Be sure to provide appropriate guidance and support for students while they engage in repeated readings.

Phrased (syntactically appropriate) reading. Teach students to read text in syntactically appropriate and meaningful chunks or phrases (e.g., nouns, verbs, prepositional phrases). Help them to see that a reader's voice can mark phrase boundaries while reading orally.

Awareness of text difficulty level. When students are reading without assistance, provide them with independent-level materials. When students have an opportunity to practice and rehearse, you may challenge them with materials that are somewhat more difficult, even at the frustration level. With supported and repeated practice using the principles above, students can learn to master even challenging materials.

Synergy. Create synergistic fluency instruction through using some or all of the techniques and principles mentioned above.

The chapters are not long. You should be able to read and respond to each one in a little more than an hour—so one or two chapters per week is a very viable approach to covering the book. In addition to reading the chapters, you will want to make time to share your own approaches and successes in teaching students to read fluently. You may wish also to invite in a teacher from your own school or a school nearby who is doing some interesting, innovative, and effective fluency instruction to share what she or he is doing, or share videotaped examples of instruction in fluency that you think are worthy of analysis and discussion. You might even want to try out some of the activities described in the book within your discussion group! Have a poetry party, engage in assessing one another's reading fluency, or perform a Readers Theater script for an audience of fellow teachers or students in your school. Be sure to think about how you and your colleagues responded to these opportunities when you are planning for fluency instruction with your own students.

Finally, as teachers dedicated to the improvement of education at your school and beyond, ask yourself, What is going to happen as a result of my (our) reading this book? What will you do differently as an individual teacher and as a group of teachers? Make plans for change, for giving fluency instruction an important role in your school's literacy curriculum. Maybe the changes you make will be baby steps. That's fine. Sometimes the most effective change happens in small increments. Also ask yourself, How will I assess, monitor, and report on whatever changes I decide to make? How will I determine success in my fluency instruction initiative? In this age of increasing accountability, we need to be sure that class time is spent in ways that make a positive difference in students' lives.

We hope that after reading this book you are as enthusiastic about reading fluency for readers in grade 5 and beyond as we are. Fluency is not the answer to every student's reading challenges. And fluency instruction can manifest itself in ways that are neither engaging nor effective. However, if done well, fluency instruction can make a huge difference in the lives of students who are not yet engaged readers, children who may otherwise fall through the cracks. It can also be enormously satisfying for teachers to lead students to texts that they may not otherwise read, to have an impact in content areas besides the language arts, and to develop reading proficiency and reading fluency without using a scripted program. Authentic and engaging fluency instruction needs to be part of an effective reading curriculum for students at all ages.

We thank you for giving us the opportunity to share the stories of the teachers portrayed in this book. We hope you find their stories helpful, and we wish you all the best on your own journey to effective reading fluency instruction.

Performing

News Broadcasts in an
Upper Elementary Classroom
in Chicago, Illinois

Timothy Rasinski (2010) cites three cornerstones of good fluency instruction: effective modeling of text, repeated reading opportunities, and supportive feedback. Practicing for performances before one's peers can enhance oral reading fluency even further, for both native speakers and English language learners (Kozub, 2000). Taking part in a performance is motivating, especially for self-aware pre-teenagers such as those in the vignette that follows. As students prepare for a performance, they work hard to compare their own performance to the model they have been shown (Stahl & Kuhn, 2002), in this case, adopting the body language and reading techniques of a television anchorperson.

Imitating the role of an anchorperson is a variation of the technique called "Say It Like the Character" (Opitz & Rasinski, 1998). In this technique, students practice reading a text, orally and silently, while trying to imagine that they are in the skin of a fictional character.

For this age group, technology gives an added dimension to the learning experience. Projects with sixth graders using new technologies indicate that they are strongly receptive to new paradigms of learning and gain valuable literacy experience, while also obtaining new skills (Bauer & Anderson, 2001; Clayton, 2000; Dockter, Haug, and Lewis, 2010).

Video technology, which many schools are adopting as it becomes more affordable, gives students immediate feedback on how they look and sound while performing. This gives students the opportunity to view their performances later—multiple times if desired—and reflect upon them. In so doing, they can improve upon their performances.

Live From Ravenswood Elementary

Tim Hart, an experienced sixth-grade teacher at Ravenswood Elementary School in Chicago, noticed that his students were always animated when it came to discussing something they'd seen on TV the previous evening. More than half of the students in

Tim's classroom are English language learners, mostly Mexican-American, who have been "mainstreamed" either after bilingual education classes or sheltered ESL classes. To these pre-adolescent students, Tim explains, textbooks can seem boring or overwhelming, whereas the media in which they immerse themselves outside of class seem endlessly interesting. One element of their media immersion is the television newscast, which is broadcast into their homes along with millions of other homes, across America every evening. In Chicago's media market, that newscast might be in English or in Spanish.

Tim observed that television anchors seemed to have perfected the skills sought in fluency instruction: smooth, accurate, and expressive reading, delivered at a conversational pace. Their delivery, he noted, is relatively similar whether the broadcast is in English or Spanish. Although anchors appear to have memorized the stories, they actually read off a teleprompter, which scrolls text down a hidden screen inside the camera lens. Anchors have poise, hold steady eye contact with the camera, and speak in a loud, clear voice. He realized that television anchors, in fact, could be considered role models for proficient oral reading.

Prior Experience in Fluency and Student Performances

For the past five years, the students in Tim's multiethnic sixth-grade class have performed operas at school as part of a partnership with Lyric Opera of Chicago. The opera company helps them learn about storytelling, how an opera is created and produced, and how to identify elements of drama, movement, and mood in music. Ravenswood's sixth graders perform a full-length opera, in costume, for the K–5 students at the school by lip-synching to recordings as a student narrator keeps the story line moving forward.

Because of this unique project, performing in front of others was nothing new for Tim's students. His newest fluency brainstorm arose two years ago, as teachers talked together two years ago about what kinds of presentations could be shared at the upcoming Family Reading Night. Tim decided to showcase student achievements in current events study through a simulated television broadcast that would be performed live for the parents from the "studio," his classroom. Thus was Ravenswood Broadcasting Company—or RBC—born.

The Lesson Plan

Tim went to the website of one of the local television network affiliates and downloaded scripts for the news, sports, weather, and commercials for that day. With help from student teacher Andrea Lancki, his kids used the Internet to find the weather forecast; for sports, they focused on the current season, which was football, "and, of course, the Bears—especially since they were doing so well!" For the news portion, Tim and Andrea wanted something that would be a little more interesting to kids, so they googled "strange news"

13

and found a story about a group of children who had witnessed a robbery and car crash. The kids memorized the licence plate number of the perpetrator by chanting it.

The teachers edited the stories for length and saved them to a Word file. Tim enlarged the type, put in blanks for the announcer names, and split the scripts into two speaking parts: Anchor 1 and Anchor 2. He then photocopied the scripts onto cardstock so that the pages would stay upright when read by students in standing positions.

Working in pairs, the students read the two-page scripts, alternating in the roles of Anchor 1 and Anchor 2. "In the beginning, they looked down at their script," Tim explains, "but we worked on how to hold the papers up and move their thumbs down to guide them as they read, so they would be able to maintain eye contact with the camera." The students practiced reading with expression and talked about what that meant.

After three days of practice, they were ready to "go live" on RBC. Tim reserved one of the school's two digital video cameras and a tripod, and his student teacher became familiar with its operation. He connected the camera to the TV in the classroom so that students would be able to see themselves on the set before the taping. "This helped them with their posture and expression," he explains.

The day before the videotaping was to take place, Tim put the scripts on large cue cards. Each "news team" started its presentation when the camera operator called out "5-4-3-2-1 ACTION!" and snapped down the "clapper." The rest of the class watched as each team was taped.

The evening of the performance was a chilly October night in Chicago. Families and neighbors gathered at Ravenswood for its annual Family Reading Night. People moved from room to room, enjoying various activities. Marlene Levin, the school's literacy coordinator, happened to drift into Tim's room. Students had dressed up for the taping session, and the school's video camera was focused on the raised stage. "I was totally blown away," she exclaims. "I hadn't heard a thing about this project, and suddenly here was a beautiful integrated unit, with students doing reading, writing, fluency practice, and public speaking. I begged him to do another live performance during the school day, so more teachers and kids could see it." They brought the show to another sixth-grade class, and shortly after that, performed it again for an all-school assembly.

After Family Reading Night, the whole class watched the footage, and pairs critiqued themselves and the other news teams, using a T-chart of "pluses and pushes." (See page 18.) Later in the week, each team had a chance to re-perform their broadcast, and they discussed their individual and team improvements, using the components of fluency and the T-chart. Later, they wrote about their performances and the whole process.

To prepare for the larger assembly, the class created a television news set, including a set of risers and an RBC banner large enough to hang behind three seated anchorpersons on the stage. Then, they brainstormed additional vignettes to be included in what they titled the "Special Winter Broadcast of the RBC—Live From Ravenswood's Winter Assembly." The students delivered the regular news, but they also went looking for their own stories. "Students worked together on writing, practicing with partners, timing, and designing their costumes. We also did a lot of practicing in the room, moving the desks aside to make it look like a stage, and some practicing on the larger stage prior to the assembly performances," explains Tim. They added "roving reporters," who were "live on the scene" at the street corner where the Ravenswood Choir was singing for a tree lighting.

After additional news, it was back to the streets again to the RBC's roving reporter, Ricky, who asked shoppers what the "hot gift items" were for that season. The Ravenswood community loved every minute of it.

Year Two and Beyond

Tim reports that during the second year, he followed the same format with his new students, except that this time, students took more responsibility. "As fifth graders, they had seen my class perform at the assembly the year before," he explains, and he showed them the videos from the previous year, which helped to orient them. "This year, the students were involved in finding information, writing the script, revising, and editing. They edited for grammar, of course, but also for time frames, understanding that TV requires quick and to-the-point information. We discussed how the speaking rate needed to be just right so that it felt conversational and not robotic, not too fast, not too slow."

Tim has even bigger plans now. "Our physical education teacher, Jeff, found some music from different news channels that I'd like to incorporate in the future. I'd also like to incorporate content area topics into the newscast, particularly math and social studies. To start, we are to going to report 'live' from an archaeological dig set up in the classroom, with a student wrapped up as a mummy!"

This year, Tim has given parents a chance to see the project with the news videos playing during report card pickup. "It's sort of like a newsletter, but a video version," he quips. The video also includes an explanation of how the Live From RBC project relates to student reading achievement.

Tim says it adds to the excitement for kids to be able to read news stories aloud from that same day. He considers this a benefit of having the Internet in the classroom—they can get fresh stories. However, it's not necessary to use the Internet. Students can also adapt, practice, and perform stories from magazines like *Scholastic News* or *Time for Kids* as well. Other sources for scripts might include history texts, biographies of scientists, student writing for other projects, screenplays, adaptations of short stories, and even recipes (for a cooking show format). Students with technical interests can read and report about auto repair or computer technology; others might create public service messages.

Evidence of Success

Beyond the school-wide attention and praise the project receives, Tim and his student teachers have noticed changes in the students when they join the RBC News Team. "They suddenly become very interested in reading the script over and over again to get it right. They are very observant of other student news teams as they deliver their reports and look for 'positives and pushes' to share. They are more aware of their volume and pacing, as the broadcast requires them to read it in this way. They realize they need to incorporate their bodies into the presentation and find ways to look up while reading."

Tim's new student teacher, Luis Diaz, observes, "The students are very meticulous and want to make it perfect." Two particular students stood out for him. One with special needs was more focused in this project than he had ever been in class. "Oh, we're going to be in front of the camera?" he asked Luis. Once he realized that, he "jumped at the opportunity and took on a leadership role." Although he struggled with the words, the rest of the group was able to help him out. "They took charge," notes Luis.

Another memorable student was Maria, who came to class speaking little English and was "shy in both languages." The class helped her out with her lines, and the RBC event provided her with her first opportunity to speak in front of the whole class. Since then, says Luis, "She has improved by leaps and bounds."

Another positive byproduct is that students have begun producing their own segments, using the format as a guide for writing. Tim explains, "Dion was excellent at finding and writing the 'strange news' section for our last broadcast. Interestingly, we later saw the same exact topic in our weekly student newsmagazine! Miguel was very interested in writing the sports section, and he worked with Jose, who has special needs, to create a fun script about the Bears season. The opening line was, 'What a difference a year makes!' Paulina and Alexandra were also added to the script for the weather report."

New vocabulary was another positive side effect. "The kids had a chance to practice new vocabulary through the repeated reading that was necessary to prepare their presentations," Tim says. "For example, students had never heard the word 'trounced,' which was used in the sports report. But by the time they performed the script, they showed their understanding by reading it with expression."

This year's RBC was a big hit on Family Reading Night, with more students and parents participating than the previous year. They taped the event, and several of the students' parents participated as news anchors along with their children.

The project has all the pillars of good fluency instruction: an opportunity to practice repeated reading with a purpose, peer work, modeling, and the chance to self-monitor. Tim adds, "Now I am trying to help them transfer the fluency practice into silent reading. I tell them, 'Keep your inside voice in your mind when you're reading.' They tell me that really helps them remember what they're reading."

Reflections

1. In Tim's project, the online transcript of a TV broadcast was turned into a script for students to practice and perform. What are some other text sources that could be used to put together a live broadcast?

2. Besides a parent open house, family reading night, or all-school assembly, what are some other occasions during the school year where a "live broadcast" could take place? What stories could "roving reporters" cover?

3. What are some ways the broadcast media theme could be further explored in the upper elementary curriculum?

4. Think of some ways this project could be adapted to be a cross-grade project. What might be some of the benefits and challenges of doing this project across grade levels? What ways might fluency practice form part of the activities for the younger grades, too?

5. After reading the vignette, what can you observe about the ways this project addresses the needs of linguistically and culturally diverse learners in particular?

6. In what ways does this project resemble having a student newspaper, and in what ways does it differ? How could a student newspaper project incorporate fluency activities?

Pluses and Pushes Self-Assessment Chart

Student Name: _____   Date: _____

	Pluses	Pluses—ways to improve
My reading rate was: ✳ Not too fast, not too slow ✳ Conversational pace		
I used expression in my ✳ reading of the text ✳ body language ✳ interaction with other anchors through nodding, etc. ✳ eye contact with camera		
I was accurate ✳ in the pronunciation of words ✳ in reading all the words		
I was attentive to volume by ✳ reading loud enough ✳ being aware of the microphone		

Assessing Reading
and *Reading Fluency*
in Mayfield, Ohio

This is the age of high-stakes testing—FCAT, OGT, SAT, TAKS, SOL, MEAP, NAEP, MCAS (to name just a few). Most often, these assessments indicate a level of student proficiency, but do not provide information to guide daily instruction. In addition, most high-stakes, standardized tests do not assess fluency, a critical skill for successful reading.

Many districts use informal reading inventories (IRIs) to gather additional information about students' strengths and needs in reading. Although the data obtained from an IRI is valid and valuable, the amount of time needed to administer such an assessment is prohibitive. It can take one to two hours to administer a full-scale IRI to a single student and at least another hour to score and interpret it.

For years, the general public, and even many educators, have downplayed the significance of informal assessments conducted by classroom teachers. Assessments must be *standardized, norm-referenced,* or *commercially published* to garner respect. Yet, most teachers can predict quite accurately before those tests are even given which children will do well, and which children will not. Informal reading assessments conducted by the professionals who spend six hours a day, five days a week, 36 weeks a year with a child can yield invaluable information to help students on their road to literacy.

Fluency Assessment—"It Was So Easy!"

It is a very good thing when a reading teacher knows the strengths, needs, and reading level of every student. But could there actually be too much of a good thing? The teachers in Mayfield, Ohio, were beginning to think so. For two years, they had been required to administer an IRI to every student three times a year. The information they received from the assessment was thorough and certainly helpful for planning instruction. The problem was that by the time the teacher spent anywhere from 45 minutes to an hour and a half assessing each child, too much precious instructional time was lost.

A **Close-Up** Look Into **15 Diverse Classrooms**

19

Eager to help, the district administration hired substitutes to give the IRI. While this freed up the teachers, it created new problems. First, it was very costly to pay for the subs. Perhaps more important, however, receiving a typed report is not the same as actually hearing a student read, listening to him answer comprehension questions, or observing them use fix-up strategies. The teachers wanted to do their own assessments and wanted results that could guide instruction, but they did not want to take large chunks of time away from instruction. Could they have it both ways?

Informal Teacher Assessment

Tammi Bender, a district literacy specialist, worked with teachers on how to assess students informally in an ongoing way. In grade-level meetings, they discussed what they observed in their readers, asked colleagues for suggestions, and talked about how to document student growth. Tammi modeled informal assessments by observing students and then sharing what she learned with the classroom teacher. The teacher, in turn, would conduct an observation and then discuss it with Tammi.

Tammi had heard about the 3-Minute Reading Assessment (Rasinski & Padak, 2004, 2005c, 2005d) and wondered if it could supplement the teachers' informal assessments. As she studied this assessment tool, she realized that, for just a few minutes per child, it would provide important information about reading fluency and comprehension. She was especially glad to see that the Multidimensional Fluency Scale (see page 23) would provide information on all components of fluency: decoding accuracy, decoding automaticity, and rate. Other fluency rating scales she had worked with only addressed words per minute. "When we as teachers only concern ourselves with rate, children become word-callers and no longer read for meaning," she says.

Tammi noticed that one difference between the informal reading inventory and the 3-Minute Reading Assessment was that the IRI questioned students about their background knowledge of the passage they were about to read. "Add 30 seconds, ask a question or two, and you've got that too if you need it," she thought. "That would be especially helpful with our large number of ESL students."

Using the 3-Minute Assessment

Tammi began by trying it out herself with a number of children. Immediately, she saw the value of the tool. "After three minutes, I could instantly walk away knowing where the child was in his reading skills and where I could take him." She listened for smoothness, phrasing, and expression. Through those fluency indicators, she was able to get a clear idea of how students were interacting with text. "Add to this the word recognition and comprehension measures the 3-Minute Reading Assessment provides," she thought, "and it could very well provide another means of assessing children that would draw upon the teacher's expertise."

Tammi took it one step at a time. "We knew that if we said, 'Here's one more thing you are required to do,' there would be some teachers who would be resistant." Instead, she rolled it out in a few classrooms where the teachers were eager to try it. She did the assessment with the first few students while the classroom teacher watched. Then the teacher assessed a student while Tammi watched. She answered any questions the teacher had and made non-judgmental suggestions. Finally, Tammi and the teacher sat side by side and each assessed students. The teacher felt assured knowing Tammi was nearby if she needed help. "They didn't need help," Tammi states. "In fact, in the beginning, some teachers thought they were doing something wrong because it was so easy."

Soon the word got out: Tammi Bender was helping some teachers do a reading test that only took a few minutes per child, and those teachers were getting some great information about their students! Tammi's phone began to ring, and the number of teachers using the 3-Minute Reading Assessment began to snowball.

Evidence of Success

"It was important for teachers to really understand fluency before assessing it," Tammi says. "We began studying fluency in our quarterly grade-level meetings at the middle school." The district purchased professional books for teachers. Several titles were chosen and each teacher received a book. The intermediate and middle school teachers studied *Still Learning to Read* (Sibberson & Szymusiak, 2003).

As the teachers became more conversant in fluency instruction and assessment, Tammi began expanding the 3-Minute Reading Assessment into other classrooms. Before long, the majority of district teachers through grade 6 were administering the assessment three times a year—fall, winter, and spring—even though they were not required to do so. In addition, many special education and ESL teachers began giving the assessment. When teachers felt they needed additional, in-depth information for a particular student who was struggling, they still had the IRI as a resource.

Tammi stresses the importance of assessing all students, not just those who are struggling. "We really want to know if we are adding value to *all* students' learning," she says. "Sometimes students who appear to be high-level readers have a fast rate but their actual comprehension is low. We found a reader could totally miss the middle of the text or the end of the text. This assessment brought it to light."

Teachers were immediately able to use the assessment results in their daily instruction using strategies they had learned in the book studies. In addition, they took results to Intervention Assistance Team meetings. Previously, when teachers were asked in team meetings what interventions they had already tried, responses were vague or predictable: "I moved her seat," "I changed his reading group," "I gave her extra help." Now, teachers talked about instruction in more focused and measurable terms: "I tried echo-reading for four weeks," "I used structured repeated reading," "We are doing Readers Theater daily."

Next Steps

Tammi Bender is now an elementary principal in Mayfield and continues to lead teachers in fluency instruction. She ordered copies of the 3-Minute Reading Assessment for every teacher in her building and provided refresher training. In addition, one staff meeting a month is devoted to discussing student progress in reading.

For too long, educators and the general public have bought into the rhetoric that claims, "Teachers don't know how to assess their students. Let the test company in Iowa (or New York or California) tell us how they are doing." When given support and provided time to share their expertise and experiences, teachers can assess reading progress, and reading fluency in particular, without relinquishing precious teaching time.

Reflections

1. In 1892, William James wrote, "The teacher's success or failure in teaching reading is based, so far as the public estimate is concerned, upon the oral reading method." What is the perception of a teacher's success or failure in teaching reading based upon today? Is that a legitimate measure? What other measures would you accept as evidence that a teacher is doing a good job of teaching students to read?

2. Many high-stakes, standardized tests do not assess fluency. Why do you think that is so?

3. Reading rate has become an important part of most fluency assessments. What do you see as the strengths and concerns related to assessing fluency through reading rate?

4. Most current fluency assessments do not include prosody. Is it important to assess prosody, or expression, in reading?

5. Does your current assessment program provide enough information about fluency? If not, how could you supplement it?

6. Role-play a parent conference in which you share results of a fluency assessment. What information will you provide? How will you help parents understand the importance of fluency?

7. How often do you think fluency should be assessed? Is it necessary to assess all students equally? Why or why not?

Multidimensional Fluency Scale*

Choose a text at or below the student's instructional level. Allow the child to read the passage silently and answer any questions about pronunciation or meaning of specific words in the passage. After this preview, ask the student to read the same passage orally. Students rated in the lower half of the scale for any of the dimensions may be at risk for fluency and overall reading proficiency.

	1	**2**	**3**	**4**
Expression and Volume	Reads in a quiet voice as if to get words out. The reading does not sound natural like talking to a friend.	Reads in a quiet voice. The reading sounds natural in part of the text, but the reader does not always sound like they are talking to a friend.	Reads with volume and expression. However, sometimes the reader slips into expressionless reading and does not sound like they are talking to a friend.	Reads with varied volume and expression. The reader sounds like they are talking to a friend with their voice matching the interpretation of the passage.
Phrasing	Reads word-by-word in a monotone voice.	Reads in two or three word phrases, not adhering to punctuation, stress and intonation.	Reads with a mixture of run-ons, mid sentence pauses for breath, and some choppiness. There is reasonable stress and intonation.	Reads with good phrasing; adhering to punctuation, stress and intonation.
Smoothness	Frequently hesitates while reading, sounds out words, and repeats words or phrases. The reader makes multiple attempts to read the same passage.	Reads with extended pauses or hesitations. The reader has many "rough spots."	Reads with occasional breaks in rhythm. The reader has difficulty with specific words and/or sentence structures.	Reads smoothly with some breaks, but self-corrects with difficult words and/ or sentence structures.
Pace	Reads slowly and laboriously.	Reads moderately slowly.	Reads fast and slow throughout reading.	Reads at a conversational pace throughout the reading.

Scores of 10 or more indicate that the student is making good progress in fluency.

Scores below 10 indicate that the student needs additional instruction in fluency.

SCORE _____

Adapted from Zutell and Rasinski (1991).

*This scale is an adaptation of a rubric developed by Zutell & Rasinski, (1991). Kimberly Monfort, a third-grade teacher at Bon View Elementary School in Ontario, California, developed the above format.

Student Fluency Rubric

A good reader works on four areas of fluency. To become a more fluent reader, I need to work on expression and volume, phrasing, smoothness, and pace.

I will receive a 4 for expression and volume if . . .

* I read with good expression and enthusiasm.
* I vary my expression and volume to match my understanding of the text.

I will receive a 4 for phrasing if . . .

* I read with good phrasing mostly in phrases and sentence units.

I will receive a 4 for smoothness if . . .

* I read smoothly with some breaks that I can change. quickly through self-corrections.

I will receive a 4 for pace if . . .

* I read consistently at a conversational pace.
* I use an appropriate rate throughout my reading.

Adapted from 3-Minute Reading Assessments by T. V. Rasinski & N. Padak (2005d).

Teacher
Fluency Modeling
in Cuyahoga Falls, Ohio

Teacher modeling is a powerful way for students to gain an internal sense of fluency, as well as improve their comprehension, vocabulary, and attitude toward reading (Rasinski, 2005). After reading aloud a short story or poem, the teacher can have a conversation with students about fluency, pointing out the volume, voice modulation, and phrasing used. She can ask students if they noted times when the reading slowed down or sped up. She can ask: What could a reader be trying to convey through a change in pace (e.g., a sense of urgency, elation, or despondence)?

Content area reading is also a great opportunity for modeling. For example, when assigning a section of the science textbook to be read for homework, a teacher can read the first paragraph or so, using appropriate expression and rate. Then, he can model strategies such as predicting what the assignment will be about or connecting the text to prior student knowledge. He can also ask the students to identify whether or not his reading was "fluent" and what that means. The conversation could conclude with instructions to apply these same strategies to the homework and to be prepared to discuss their fluent reading strategies the next day along with the content of the assignment (Fawcett & Rasinski, 2008).

Modeling Fluency: You Just Have to Hear It, and Hear It, and Hear It

Susie Greathouse is in love with language. She loves the sound of words like *carillon*, *mercurial*, and *unabashed*. She loves the cadence of Elizabeth Barrett Browning's verse. She loves the dialogue of a Robert Cormier novel. She loves the quaint language of the King James Bible.

But Susie knows that when students enter her Bolich Middle School eighth-grade classroom in the fall, most of them are definitely not in love with the language she loves. She speculates, "Because they use street talk and what I call the abbreviated language of TV and e-mail, they do not have a rich store of vocabulary words to call up."

25

Many of her students claim to hate reading, especially poetry. However, Susie has a theory about what will change their minds, and it works like magic. "It's the Susie Greathouse Theory," she says with a smile. "You learn language from the gut. You just have to hear it, and hear it, and hear it." So students hear language, and hear language, and hear language as Susie models fluent reading day in and day out.

Modeling Fluency Through Read-Alouds

"I do not ever recall seeing fluency mentioned in my teacher's manuals," Susie reflects. Even so, she believes that fluency is critical for comprehension. In order to demonstrate what comprises fluent reading, Susie reads aloud to her eighth graders as much as or more than most elementary teachers read to their young charges. It's hard to say exactly *how much* time she spends reading aloud because of the way reading aloud is woven throughout a lesson. Although Susie always does a daily read-aloud of 10 to 15 minutes, read-alouds are also scattered throughout a class period. For example, if the class is studying character development, Susie might read excerpts from three different picture books at three different times as the discussion proceeds. If they are studying setting, she might read a short story with a great setting, and later in the period, read the section describing the setting again.

She describes the various formats her read-alouds take: "I read poetry or short stories to students every day. We engage in choral reading of poetry and prose texts. They really liked Elizabeth Barrett Browning's "How Do I Love Thee?" We read dramas and engage in Readers Theater. I just read aloud with them the play version of *The Diary of Anne Frank*. They love plays! I saw this as a rich opportunity. We had a great two weeks. Often, I read the opening chapter of a book from the classroom library so they can decide if they want to choose it for Readers Workshop."

Susie's students have so many choices for Readers Workshop that her book previews are a good thing. Hundreds of books wait for their readers in baskets, on the shelves, and on tables. Although she has traditional desks, they are arranged in groups to encourage book conversations among students.

Often, Susie discusses what she did to read fluently—how she read quickly and smoothly or made her voice go up or down or soft and loud to enhance the listener's understanding. Sometimes, she talks about the vocabulary words in the text and stresses how important automatic word recognition is for fluent reading. Usually, however, she uses her natural ability to connect students and language through her obvious enjoyment of the reading. Susie's modeling is so captivating that it doesn't always need an explanation.

Modeling Fluency Through Poetry

Recently, while reflecting on her curriculum, Susie was surprised by something. "I didn't realize how much poetry I use," she said. "Although many of the students will say they hate poetry, when I read it aloud, they love it." Susie has a dramatic flair that commands the attention of even the most reluctant reader. Students can't help but notice how volume and intonation capture their imaginations. Students can be seen affectionately imitating Susie's expressions in the hallways or cafeteria.

One year's students especially loved the great classic poem "The Creation" by James Weldon Johnson (1922). Susie read the poem several times so the students could hear how it should sound when read fluently. "They *loved* that line, 'And God said, That's good!' " Susie told us, repeating the line with such expression that we could easily see why. "I was in tears when they did it this year," she confessed. Then, the class read the poem in parts; one student read line 1, another line 2, and so on.

What has been especially gratifying is how the young men in her classes respond to poetry. Many of them she refers to as "boys in crisis." They cannot or will not read. Susie hooks them by reading aloud parts of Jacqueline Woodson's book *Locomotion* (2004). The story is about Lonnie, a young boy whose class is learning to write poetry. For the first time, Lonnie is finding words to tell the world about his family, the fire that took his parents away, his little sister, and his world. "The book is short enough that it is accessible to students," Susie observes. "They look at the print on the page and they feel they can get through it. This book really is about an inner sense of language."

Modeling Fluency by Singing the Blues

When Susie sings the blues, it is fluency modeling at its best. On the first day of the blues unit, the students are amused when Susie stands up, begins snapping her fingers to the beat of the blues poem "Catcher Sings the Blues" (Janeczko, 2000, p. 59), and makes a soft noise: chih-chih chih-chih-chih

As she continues to snap and sway, she says, "You gotta get the rhythm, kids." Soon the students are swaying and snapping along, and Susie substitutes words of the poem into the rhythm:

> Crouching low, I sing the blues
> The aches are now a part of me
> Blocking home, I sing the blues
> O, the aches are now a part of me
> Bruises, bumps, and scrapes
> Have worn me down, can't you see?

Fluency is critical for a genre like the blues, and Susie's students both hear it *and* feel it. Throughout the unit, Susie draws on *Teaching 10 Fabulous Forms of Poetry* (Janeczko, 2000). The book models forms of poetry and includes reproducibles and worksheets. "It's a neat resource for teachers," Susie says simply. Students keep their own blues folders where they summarize what they are learning about the history of the blues

Teacher Poem: *My Teacher*

My teacher sings the blues
She sings them in her room
My teacher sings the blues
She sings them in her room
And dances on her feet
Expressing her students' gloom.

She sings child, child, child
I love you; I do try
She sings child, child, child
I love you; I do try
But my hope is for your future
I want you to touch the sky.

My teacher sings the blues
She sings them in her room
My teacher sings the blues
She sings them in her room
She ain't never joined a rock band
But her songs shout when learning blooms!

—*Susan E. Greathouse*

and the lives of famous blues artists.

The most exciting entries in the folders are the students' own blues poems. As with everything else, Susie models writing blues lyrics by sharing her own writing.

For an entire week, students write blues poems during Readers-Writers Workshop. Susie grades them with a rubric she created. However, even the best of rubrics could not capture the significance of some of the blues poems students write. Samantha wrote about her mother who recently passed away. Josh shared the trials he faced with a malignant brain tumor. Britney wrote about the flames that consumed her family's home one night.

Susie and the students celebrate the culmination of the unit with a "Blues Coffee House," complete with Principal McBurney on guitar and Assistant Principal Musat on bongo drums.

Student Poem: *The Missing Her Blues*

An empty closet, with only a pair of shoes
I'm still singing the missing her blues
A year and a half later
And I remember her smell, and hugs
And the way to us she catered

My mother was so full of life
Which was taken away too soon
Now I look up at the sky
And see her among the stars and the moon

She loved my brother and I a lot
But her laugh is something I've almost forgot
The memory of her still lingers
And I still remember her beautiful face
As I clutch her picture between my fingers

An empty closet, with only a pair of shoes
I'm still singing the missing her blues
I love you forever, Mom, you know that
I promise I'll see you in heaven, for that is a fact

— *Samantha S.*

Student Poem: *The Fire Blues*

I saw the flames with my own eyes
It took all the pictures and memories in disguise
I felt the fire under my feet
As I tried to escape the deadly heat.

I have the fire blues.
It took away what was rightfully ours and
Forced us to move.
Now we don't know what to do.
I have the fire blues.

Everyone tried to help
But it didn't stop the pain
And during the lonely nights the tears
Flowed down my cheeks like rain.
I have the fire blues.

I saw the flames with my own eyes
It took all the pictures and memories in disguise
Now my family has to start fresh
But I think together we can make the best
Out of this horrible mess
I have the fire blues.

—*Britney M.*

Evidence of Success

Susie is the teacher of record for 124 reading students. Because her philosophy focuses on assessing fluency in the context of authentic texts, as opposed to tests, which isolate fluency as a separate skill, she looks in many places for evidence that reading fluency is improving. One such piece of evidence is students' journals. "Quality of written response is, I believe, evidence of acquired fluency," she explains. "If they cannot read fluently, it shows in the number of books they read and log into their journals. If they are accustomed to reading and hearing fluency, their own writing will reflect that."

Susie uses a rubric to grade students' journals that includes number of books read, appropriateness of titles for an individual's reading level, and quality of paragraph structure, sentence structure, vocabulary, and use of mechanics. A recent year's final journal grades showed evidence of fluency. Out of 124 students, 99 students earned a C or higher. And 36 students earned an A.

However, Susie is keenly aware that letter grades are but one measure of student growth. "Growth in fluency can also be measured in the shared life of the learning community in a classroom," she notes. The following story of Gerald is just one of hundreds of such stories she has gathered over the years, evidence of success that doesn't require numbers. Susie explains:

"Gerald walked into my reading/writing eighth-grade class in the fall. The first thing I noticed about Gerald was that he was small and chubby, he had a beautiful smile, and his hands were the size and shape of a 6-year-old's. Gerald could barely hold a pencil, and his writing was almost illegible. He rarely read, did not understand paragraph structure, and was filled with school anxiety.

I reflected on how I might help him. First, I assigned Gerald only short stories with readability at fourth/fifth grade. After Gerald read a story, I would call him to the conference table and ask a very specific question, for example, 'What was the problem faced by the main character?' Then I would say, 'Just talk to me, Gerald. I will write down what you say.' I modeled how to write a topic sentence, and then I scribed his ideas. We moved from this process to my writing a sentence and Gerald writing a sentence. We worked together for months. Gerald started using the computer for his writing. By the end of the year, he was choosing to read books like Louis Sachar's *Holes* (2000).

Of course, there were students at the other extreme. As we continued to read fiction and nonfiction together, I modeled writing by sharing examples of my own writing, as well as my own reading. I watched several of my eighth graders move from readers of adolescent fiction to readers of adult fiction. By the end of the school year, here are some of the titles I was seeing: Sue Monk Kidd's *The Secret Life of Bees*, *The Lovely Bones* by Alice Sebold, *Until We Meet Again* by Michael Korenblit, Margaret Mitchell's *Gone With the Wind*, and Michael Crichton's *Prey*.

Susie Greathouse models fluency daily through language, reading, and writing. Her students "just hear it, and hear it, and hear it." She concludes, "Fluency may be defined as having facility in the use of language, but a reading teacher knows that fluent readers are present in her classroom when students open the books they have chosen and fall in!"

Reflections

1. Describe the nature of your read-alouds (e.g., How often do you read aloud? What do you read aloud? How do the students respond? Are you satisfied with what you do?)

2. Read a short passage aloud to yourself. Make notes about how you could describe your fluency with this passage to students.

3. The blues is a unique unit for teaching fluency. Can you think of other genres that are not in the standard language arts curriculum that could increase fluency?

4. Susie Greathouse shared her theory of language learning in this chapter. Can you articulate your theory of how students become fluent readers?

5. Do you think electronic communication, street talk, and television affect your students' language learning? If so, how?

6-Point Rubric for Journal Evaluation

6 ALL WORKSHOP REQUIREMENTS ARE MET. 93%–100%

Journal entries are focused on prompt. Writing is well organized and includes supporting details from the text. Vocabulary and word usage is appropriate. Errors in sentence structure, spelling, punctuation, and capitalization are few. Book choices are appropriate, and booklist is updated.

5 MOST WORKSHOP REQUIREMENTS ARE MET. 85%–92%

Writing is focused and contains some supporting details. Vocabulary and word usage is good. Vocabulary is appropriate but may not always be the best choice. Some errors in sentence structure, spelling, punctuation, and capitalization. Book choices are good, and booklist is updated.

4 SOME WORKSHOP REQUIREMENTS ARE MET. 73%–84%

Writing is generally related to the prompt but lacks enough details to give support. Paragraph organization is weak. Vocabulary is limited and predictable. Errors in sentence structure, spelling, punctuation, and capitalization show that knowledge of correct usage is inconsistent. Book choices are fair, and booklist is incomplete.

3 FEW WORKSHOP REQUIREMENTS ARE MET. 65%–72%

Writing shows an awareness of prompt but details are unrelated. Writing is not organized. Vocabulary is limited and word choices lack purpose. Errors in sentence structure, spelling, punctuation, and capitalization interfere with understanding. Book choices are poor, and booklist is incomplete.

2 WORKSHOP REQUIREMENTS ARE NOT MET. 58%–64%

Writing shows only a slight awareness of the prompt. Sentence structure is simplistic, vocabulary is limited, and errors in sentence structure, spelling, punctuation, and capitalization limit understanding. Book choices are poor, and booklist is incomplete.

1 WORKSHOP REQUIREMENTS ARE NOT MET. 57% or below

Writing shows little awareness of the prompt and has no logical organization or sentence structure. Vocabulary is very limited. Errors in sentence structure, spelling, punctuation, and capitalization show that knowledge of correct usage is very limited. Book choices are poor, and booklist is incomplete.

A Community of Learners

in New South Wales, Australia

In recent years, the phrase *community of learners* has worked its way into our ever-expanding educational lexicon. A Google search of the phrase "classroom as community of learners" yields 1,900,000 hits. And is it any wonder? No one would argue with the need for a positive classroom climate, mutual goals, shared responsibility, individual rights, and interdependence—just a few of the many terms associated with a learning community. In a community, everyone belongs, and in Maslow's hierarchy of needs, belonging is just one notch below survival and safety (Woolfolk, 2004). Teachers of adolescents might argue that belonging often supersedes safety and in some cases it even trumps survival.

Establishing a learning community usually begins with conversations about social issues such as behavior, respect, and democracy. These expectations are then applied to academic contexts such as cooperative learning, projects, literature circles, and class discussions. However, teachers should not overlook the potential to develop a community of learners within the context of fluency instruction. A strong sense of community is important for fluency development, especially for struggling readers, since fluency instruction most often involves oral reading. Christensen (1994, p. 50) notes that "to become a community, students must learn to live in someone else's skin, understand the parallels of hurt, struggle and joy across class and culture lines and work for change. For that to happen, students need more than an upbeat, supportive teacher; they need a curriculum that teaches them how to empathize with others."

A Journey to Teaching

Monique Frangi had a successful consultancy business that allowed her to use her passion for language in the publishing field. But she wasn't happy. Monique explains:

> "I had become deeply disillusioned with the pursuit of profit. The only contribution I was making was to increase the bottom line for clients. I

needed to feed my soul. I had always thought that if I did not have to work for a living, I'd do volunteer work with children. So I became a teacher and, on Australian teachers' salaries, this is as close to volunteer work as you can get!

When Monique stepped into her classroom at Muirfield High School in New South Wales, Australia, she carried with her an interest in language, an affinity for children with learning disabilities and behavioral issues, and a sense of social responsibility. With her assignment to teach English to secondary students, the stage was set for reading fluency within the context of a community of learners.

Establishing a Learning Community

Monique's English classes overflow with reading activities—sustained silent reading, teacher read-alouds, student independent reading, and reading lessons. This context provides many opportunities for Monique to model and discuss the importance of fluency. The English curriculum also includes public speaking and drama; Monique believes those areas are important in fluency development for adolescent learners as well. When preparing a speech, they must read to research their topic and then read their note cards and quotes throughout the presentation. Drama requires students to read scripts with automaticity and expression. They must chunk words into phrases, know where to pause, and know where to place emphasis. Monique shares:

> Most students think if they know how to read, then that's good enough. This is particularly true of students with low motivation. However, the reason we push fluency is that it is directly connected to confidence and self-esteem. With fluency, not only do students come across more confidently, but they actually feel more confident. In drama, this is half the battle. Developing fluency is particularly important for students challenged with learning or behavioral difficulties, since they struggle to engage.

Monique will spend as much time as necessary to establish rules of the learning environment. "The single most important element in developing fluency in the classroom is to foster a safe and supportive learning environment," says Monique. "How many of you are afraid of this assignment?" Monique recently asked an eighth-grade class preparing for their first speech. There were nervous giggles, and a few hands went up. "Stephanie, what about you? Tell us how you are feeling about this assignment." Stephanie readily admitted she was nervous. Monique probed, "What makes you nervous? What do you think people are thinking as you perform, speak?" "I'm afraid they'll laugh," Stephanie responded, and with that the lesson went into full swing. Allowing students to voice their fears is an important step in building community. Once the first student speaks out, others are open to sharing their concerns as well. They feel connected; they are not alone in the way they feel. Monique later reflected on the process:

> At heart, the students are afraid of criticism, which gets right down to kids' basic need to belong and be accepted. This is a typical lesson. We have a discussion and everyone gets to speak. Once we establish that everyone in the class feels the same, we establish the ground rules: We support each other, we don't criticize or make fun of each other, and we all benefit.

Monique likens teaching to theater, and she uses high drama to demonstrate what a classroom community *is* and *is not*. She begins to fidget. Within the time span of a few minutes, she checks her fingernails, plays with her cell phone, jots a few notes, stares off into space, looks around the room, slumps in her chair, and finally puts her head on the desk.

"How will you feel if I do this while you're speaking?" Monique asks. "Will you worry that I'm not listening? That I think it's boring? How will that affect your confidence in your speech/performance?" The class then discusses active listening.

Students think of ways they can support one another. For example, they might talk about nonverbal support like nodding, or smiling, or simply keeping eye contact. (See the chart on page 38.) They explore what support looks like in the way the head is positioned, eyes are directed, or body is postured (upright, perhaps with a forward lean toward the speaker). Monique contrasts this with the distracting behaviors she demonstrated earlier. "This is what we want of an audience when we perform/speak," she tells the class. "Therefore, this is *your* responsibility as an audience when you are listening to the efforts of your peers. If each of us does this, and supports each other, we'll generate maximum confidence and ease for each student performing."

Monique also looks for ways to give ownership. One way is by asking students to come up with their own rubric for the assessment of presentations. They work on this in groups and they fine-tune it as a class until they have a final document. This process means that the students have actively thought about what constitutes a top performance and that they have an opportunity to discuss expectations and techniques before the assessment. Often, Monique has students use the class-generated rubric for peer assessment. This, again, compels discussion about empathy, positive criticism, mutual support, and respect. Most students approach the responsibility of peer assessment very seriously and sensitively. Once again, they have invested in building classroom community.

Monique acknowledges that certain students can neither sit still nor focus for an extended length of time. She gives them the option of staying for each performance and showing support or going to the library to study. If they stay and meet, or partially meet, standards of active listening, they get a merit (which can lead to a certificate of achievement from the head teacher later) or similar acknowledgement of their effort. If they choose to go to the library as an alternative, this is respected and not held against them. "I need to understand that asking some students to sit quietly and at attention for an extended period is setting them up to fail. By this stage, a sense of group experience is developing and most students will want to stay," Monique explains.

Theatrics in Fluency Instruction

Once Monique and her students have established the rules of mutual support and respect, direct fluency instruction begins. Once again, Monique resorts to theatrics as she monotones a speech on the state economy. "Well, what do you think?" she asks. "Full marks?" A lively discussion ensues about reading with expression, a centerpiece of reading fluency. Monique assures her students that expressive reading easily transfers to expressive public speaking.

"Well, then, how about this?" she asks, and proceeds to deliver a speech about computer games at a rapid-fire pace. Now, students complain that she is talking too fast. Monique has set the stage to present another important component of reading fluency—pace. She tells the students:

> Pace is really important in creating interest. I'm now going to talk to you about computer games, and I've got some really important things to say. 'Computer games are enormous fun and one can sit in front of them for hours being highly entertained [*she slows her voice*], however, this can have negative consequences [*slows voice again*].'

Monique points out how she drew their attention to *negative consequences* by slowing her voice. She also points out how her pace varied in this short statement, which makes it more interesting. She then introduces the use of dramatic pause for emphasis, a reading fluency skill that will transfer to their public speaking assignment.

On another day, Monique might pick up a story by Paul Jennings, an award-winning Australian author of young adult literature, and start reading without phrasing. She asks the class, "Can you tell if I understand what I'm reading? I can obviously read the words okay. I can do that well because I've learned phonics and how to decode words. But, can you tell if I understand the meaning of the words or what's happening in the relationship between the two characters?" She reads the excerpt again with appropriate phrasing, and asks if it's now clearer to them as listeners. "If you can understand from my reading what's going on, then you know I do, too," she says, and then explains how phrasing, or "chunking," facilitates comprehension.

Once a safe environment is established and students have a good understanding of what reading fluency sounds like, Monique provides regular opportunities for students to read aloud in class. Sometimes it is a story, sometimes a textbook; another time, it might be instructions for an assignment. Students follow along in their own texts as their classmates read aloud. During daily silent reading, she works with individual students who struggle with reading fluency. She notes, "Individual praise and guidance builds their confidence for those occasions when they are called upon to read aloud in front of the class." In addition, three or four times a term, Monique makes notes on students' oral reading in class.

Evidence of Success

Although Monique was a first-year teacher at this writing and felt "the stories are to come," she was able to share examples of success. Roxy, a ninth-grade drama student, is a shy girl who finds performing in front of others terrifying but fun. In the past, the terror took over and Roxy's performances were marked by a lack of movement and expression. Roxy was part of a small group asked to perform a *commedia dell'arte* scenario, an Italian comedy art form, for Muirfield's performance night, which is designed to showcase for parents what the students are achieving in dramatic arts. The process of rehearsal in both voice and movement in Monique's class paid off, though, and Roxy's performance was a great success. In her reflective journal, Roxy wrote that the biggest lesson she learned was that it was okay to take a risk and challenge herself in front of others.

Monique has observed the development of student confidence and self-esteem demonstrated by increased participation and risk-taking. Reading grades have improved for many students, and there is an increased willingness to read aloud from texts in class.

Monique Frangi recognizes the power of reading fluency to build self-confidence. She also knows that oral reading fluency is a critical prerequisite for drama and public speaking. However, she is wise enough to recognize the importance of a supportive classroom community. "If it's an unsafe environment, they'll never be able to build confidence, and they'll never build fluency," she says with certainty. Sometimes Monique demonstrates intonation, pace, and rate with the Shakespeare monologue that begins, "All the world's a stage." And she believes it! For students who are confident and fluent readers, there's no limit—all the world *can* be a stage!

Reflections

1. What literacy practices most require a "community of learners"?

2. How does the teacher's role in a community of learners differ from the teacher's role in a traditional classroom?

3. Can you think of other reading activities that involve fluency and also offer opportunities to build community in the classroom?

4. Monique uses incidental experiences in the classroom to foster fluency (e.g., reading directions). What are some other incidental experiences that can be used to foster fluency?

5. What are some obstacles to building a classroom community of learners?

6. How can those obstacles be overcome?

7. How do you model reading fluency with your students?

8. Many older students still experience difficulty in reading. How can you respond to students' reading in ways that are honest and supportive?

The Art of Public Speaking
What Makes a Good Presentation?

SPEECH

Content

It contains information that people need. However, the speaker must be mindful of how much information the audience can absorb in one sitting.

Structure

It has a logical beginning, middle, and end. It must be sequenced and paced so that the audience can understand it. The speaker must be careful not to lose the audience by wandering too far from the main point of the presentation.

Human Element

A good presentation will be remembered much more than a good report because it has a person attached to it.

Know Your Audience

You must know the composition of your audience, and gauge their initial attitudes about your topic in order for you to decide upon which approach you will take in your presentation.

VOICE

Volume

The goal is to be heard without shouting. Good speakers lower their voice to draw the audience in, and raise it to make a point.

Tone

An airplane has a different sound than leaves being rustled by the wind. A voice that carries fear can frighten the audience, while a voice that carries laughter can get the audience to smile.

Modulation/Intonation

One of the major criticisms of speakers is that they speak in a monotone voice. People report that they learn less and lose interest more quickly when listening to those who have not learned to modulate their voices.

Pace

Talking too fast causes the words and syllables to be short, while talking slowly lengthens them. Varying the pace helps to maintain the audience's interest.

BODY

Eye Contact

Speakers who make eye contact open the flow of communication and convey interest, concern, warmth, and credibility. It signals interest in others and increases the speaker's credibility.

Facial Expression

Smiling encourages your audience to perceive you as likeable, friendly, warm, and approachable. They will be more comfortable around you and will want to listen to you more.

Gestures

A lively speaking style captures attention, makes the material more interesting, and facilitates understanding.

Posture and Body Orientation

You communicate numerous messages by the way you talk and move. Standing erect and leaning forward communicates that you are approachable, receptive, and friendly. Speaking with your back turned or looking at the floor or ceiling communicates disinterest.

Nerves

The main enemy of a presenter is tension, which ruins the voice, posture, and spontaneity. The voice becomes higher as the throat tenses. Shoulders tighten up and limit flexibility, while the legs start to shake and cause unsteadiness. The presentation becomes stilted, as the speaker locks in on the notes and starts to read directly from them.

Do not fight nerves, welcome them! Then you can get on with the presentation. Nerves add to the value of the performance because adrenaline starts to kick in. If you welcome nerves, then the presentation becomes a challenge and you become better.

Using Picture Books
to Travel Through Space and Time
in Peru, New York

> To comprehend, a reader must continually construct meaning while processing an extended text. Readers keep the meaning of the whole text in mind, and this process varies with the kinds of texts they read.
>
> (Fountas & Pinnell, 2001, p. 306)

As teachers, we can learn a great deal from the quote above. Many other experts in the field of literacy (Frank Smith, P. David Pearson, Ken Goodman, Yetta Goodman, and Stephen Krashen, to name a few) support a "constructivist" approach as well. Our challenge is to envision three-dimensional, dynamic images of this approach in classrooms. We could start with an examination of content area reading.

Children encounter more and more challenging material as they progress through the grades. Without comprehension, content area reading is an exercise in futility. Classroom activities that focus on the development of fluency can provide opportunities for learners to actively construct meaning from informational text. To move toward comprehension through fluency, we need an approach that includes four essential components:

* Models of fluent reading behavior

* Reading materials that are well within the reader's instructional range

* Texts that provide natural language patterns that can be read with fluency and expression

* Opportunities to establish and practice fluency by multiple readings of familiar texts

    (Zutell & Rasinski, 1991, p. 216)

A Close-Up Look Into **15 Diverse Classrooms**

39

The following chapter describes a two-day activity that took place in November 2007. As a record of a complex situation (Ackland, 1999), it aims to provide a detailed, insider's view of the instructional decisions made by a reading specialist and a classroom teacher working with a group of fifth graders. The reading specialist, Bob Ackland, has written this account.

Bringing Meaning to Social Studies Test Prep

Mike Korth teaches fifth grade in the small town of Peru, New York, nestled among the Adirondack Mountains. Mike asked a former professor of his, Bob Ackland, to come to his classroom to help students read picture books aloud to their peers. He figured that this would be a meaningful preparation for a mandated fifth-grade social studies test given every November. Bob, a reading specialist who is a former coordinator of the graduate literacy program at the State University of New York at Plattsburgh, gathered a large number of books and arranged to visit Mike's school for a few days.

Mike faces a challenge familiar to many teachers. He doesn't want to teach to the test. But, of course, he does want his students to succeed on standardized tests. He simply believes the best way to do that is by helping these 11-year-olds develop a strong understanding of concepts in social studies. During the four years that Mike has been a teacher, his students have scored well on the tests, but Mike is always looking for new approaches.

"The class I took last summer with Dr. Caroline Knight made me think about using picture books with fifth graders," Mike declared when he met with Bob prior to the visit. "You know, a lot of picture books are written with fairly difficult text—many of them deal with sophisticated topics that my students could benefit from. I have a young group of fifth graders this year. I don't think they're ready for literature circles (Daniels, 1994) using chapter books right now, so maybe picture books could get them started."

A key to the success of this project, Mike and Bob knew, would be the quality of the reading materials. Four social studies topics emerged within the large assortment of hardbound copies of picture books (see page 49): economics, geography, history, and immigration.

Getting Started

Ways to Approach Difficult Vocabulary

Day 1: *Tuesday (instructional time: 40 minutes)*

9:20–10:00—Social Studies (introduction to picture books; models of reading strategies and presentation formats; free reading of picture books)

Mike has arranged the students' desks in two wide horseshoe shapes facing the whiteboard. This forms a small open area in the front of the room for presentations. Bob stands in that area, with a crate of more than 50 picture books on the table in front of him.

"Here's a great book," Bob says, pulling *Tikal* by Elizabeth Mann (2002) out of the crate. "As you can see, this book has full pages of printed text next to amazing drawings. Any idea what this book is about?" he asks, showing the front cover.

"That looks like a pyramid," offers one student.

"Maybe it's about Egypt," says a student in the back of the room.

To honor this brave hypothesis, Bob takes the book closer to that student and says, "You're right, Egypt did have pyramids, but this book is about a group of people who lived in what we now call Mexico."

"Is it about the Maya?" the student suggests.

"Yes! Let me read you a few lines from a page about halfway through the book: 'That leader was Hasaw Chan K'awil. He was the son of Shield Skull, the last of the four *ahuas* who had ruled Tikal in the time of darkness.'" (p. 18)

Bob looks at the students. "I'm not sure if I pronounced that right. I'm not even sure I understood what those sentences meant. I often have to read things a few times before I understand them."

After reading the sentences to the students again, he continues to think aloud. "There was a word in there that I've never seen before. It's in italics, so it might be from another language."

Bob writes *ahuas* on the whiteboard, says it aloud, and reads the second sentence another time. "How could we figure out what *ahuas* means?"

"I think it means 'leaders,' because it says they ruled Tikal," suggests one student.

As often happens in classroom interactions, a learner has jumped right over a process-oriented question and given an answer to the real, substantive question. Bob knows that it is his responsibility, as a teacher, to both honor the student's response and draw attention to a reading strategy that can be used in the future. "You're probably right," he indicates. "I think it does mean 'leaders.' Part of the sentence says 'the last of the four *ahuas* who had ruled Tikal.' It sounds like your class has already talked about how to use context to figure out words you haven't see before."

Bob gestures at the crate in front of him. "There will be words in these books that you'll need to pin down by using the meaning of the text around them," he says. "Oh, and sometimes books have glossaries. They are usually at the end of the book. Let's see. Here it is: It says *ahua* means 'king'—we were pretty close when we said 'leader.' I wish the author had told us how to pronounce that word correctly."

"Before I show you another book, take a look at this four-page foldout that shows what the city of Tikal looked like in 700 A.D., says Bob." Their eyes open wide as they see the detailed representations of multiple pyramids. "We can travel all over the world with books. I've brought you a world map that was sent to me by UNICEF. We can put pins on it to track where the books are from. Oh, one more thing," Bob remembers to point out. "We can also travel through time with picture books. We've just visited a place that existed 1,300 years ago, and we didn't even have to leave the classroom.

"The book we just looked at, *Tikal*, is related to both geography and history. All of the books in this crate have something to do with social studies," he says. "There are many different kinds of books, so in a few minutes, you'll have a chance to explore the collection." He continues, "Some of the books have very complex text—you know, long sentences, new vocabulary, big sections of print—like in *Tikal*. Other books have text that may not be so hard to understand, but the information is still very important and, I think, very interesting."

Providing Models of Fluent Oral Reading

"Here's a book about visiting an apple orchard," Bob says, holding up a copy of *One Green Apple* by Eve Bunting (2006). "I know you have orchards pretty much right across the street from the school. But imagine what it would be like to go to an orchard for the very first time. The main character in this book is named Farah. She has just arrived in the United States from another country and she's starting to learn how to speak English. This is…" Bob looks into the book to model how a reader checks for accuracy. "this is her second day at the school and her class is going on a field trip to an apple orchard.

"Mr. Korth, would you mind coming up here and reading this book to the class with me?" All eyes go to the back of the room where Mike has been watching the activity. He and Bob had not planned all of the details regarding how they would provide models of fluent reading—professionals who work together in classrooms never have time to think of everything beforehand, so one of the keys to team teaching is the ability to go with the flow. Besides, how could educators respond to teachable moments if everything was too rigidly scripted?

As Mike walks to the whiteboard, Bob tells the students that there are many ways to present books to a class. Then Bob asks Mike, "How about if I read one sentence and you read the next?"

"That sounds fine," Mike replies. "We call that 'sentence tag' in this room. I learned to call it that when I took a college class from you."

"Well, I'm glad your students know about sentence tag," says Bob. "I like to use that in small groups. Sometimes it's fun to do 'word tag' with two or three students, but that gets a little distracting because it takes people's minds away from the meaning of the material. If two people want to share a book with each other or with a larger group, they can do 'paragraph tag' or 'page tag.'

"With long books, like *Tikal*, it might be a good idea to pick particular paragraphs or pages to read out loud. It's important to have a chance to practice before people are asked to read in front of a big audience. Sometimes we can summarize the rest of the book after reading part of it," he says. "But now, Mr. Korth and I will do some sentence tag with this book about Farah's first visit to an apple orchard. How about if we always start a presentation of a book in this class by telling everyone the title of the book and then saying the names of the author and illustrator?"

Mike shows the cover to the class. "This book is called *One Green Apple*. It was written by Eve Bunting, and illustrated by Ted Lewin." Mike and Bob start reading the book to the class using sentence tag. On page five, Bob reads: "Mothers drive us to the start of an orchard where a hay wagon is waiting." Mike reads: "We climb on and lean against the bundles of hay."

Bob looks up from the book and says to the class: "Did you notice how Mr. Korth slowed down when he read 'We climb on and lean against the bundles of hay' so you could picture that in your mind? A reader often tries to help you see things with your mind's eye (Zeigler & Johns, 2005).

"What if he had read it very quickly?" Bob gestures to Mike. Knowing exactly what his colleague is suggesting, Mike uses a monotone voice to speed-read the sentence as fast as he can. When the children's laughter dies down, Bob says, "If he had read it like that the first time, we would have had trouble feeling what it would be like to be in that wagon. Mr. Korth and I will do our best to read with expression. We'll use pauses and pay attention to punctuation so that you can understand what the author wrote. Reading with expression—reading with good prosody—helps people comprehend what is going on." (Bob figures it's not too early for the fifth graders to hear words like *prosody*—making terms and strategies explicit can be beneficial for students who take responsibility for their own learning.)

"I'm guessing that a lot of you know what hay wagons and bales of hay look like. In case you don't, we will be sure to show you the illustrations. That's why picture books are so great—they give you images that are connected to the meaning of the book," he says. "If you were up in front of the class, presenting this book, you could decide when to show the illustrations and when to read the words. The important thing is this: The reader must help the listeners make sense of the text.

"I want you to pay attention to the way Mr. Korth and I are reading this book. During the next few days, we are going to ask all of you to select books and read them out loud to the class. You'll be doing this in small groups, and you'll be able to pick the book you want to read," Bob says. "Mr. Korth and I will read one more page of *One Green Apple* to demonstrate using sentence tag, but remember, there are several ways to divide up a book and read it to the class. You'll have plenty of time to decide how you want to do the presentation and to practice reading out loud."

Mike and Bob resume their reading. At one point, Bob makes a mistake and has to reread a few words. He decides to take advantage of this teachable moment. "That's called self-correcting," Bob explains. "It's okay to make mistakes, especially the first few times you read something out loud. Everyone makes mistakes—good readers go back and self-correct if the miscue has changed the meaning of the text (Goodman & Marek, 1996). If you find that you have read something that doesn't make sense, it's a good idea to read it again so that your audience will get the right meaning."

Students Provide Models for One Another

Bob rummages through the crate. "Picture books can represent many types, or genres, of literature. *Tikal* is an informational book. *One Green Apple* is a narrative. Here is a book from a different genre—poetry. This book, called *Confetti* [1996], is a collection of poems from the southwestern part of the United States. The poems were written by Pat Mora, and they sometimes use words in Spanish as well as words in English.

"There are some great ways to share poetry aloud. You may know about choral reading. The readers can decide to overlap so that more than one person says some of the words or phrases. Sometimes a reader is responsible for saying only the verbs or the first few words of each line. There are many choices that can be made.

"Instead of hearing me read part of a poem, are there any of you who would like to read a few lines?"

Fortunately, one girl raises her hand. Bob gives her *Confetti* and asks her to flip through the pages and pick any poem she'd like. The students sitting next to her volunteer to help her out. Within a few minutes, the three of them give a wonderful rendition of the first lines of "Can I, Can I Catch the Wind" (p. 12)—voicing some words in unison and making us all feel as if a breeze had entered the room:

> Can I, can I catch the wind, in the morning, catch the wind?
> Can I, can I catch the wind, in my two hands, catch the wind?
> Can I, can I catch the wind, in my basket, catch the wind?

Bob looks at the clock. Knowing that there are only 10 minutes left in today's lesson, he thanks the girls for doing such a nice job with the poem. Then Bob reaches into the crate, grabs a handful of books, and starts putting two books on each student's desk. Mike helps pass them out, happy that there are enough books so that no one feels compelled to read a particular one. Every once in a while, Bob holds up a book and says something about it. "This book, *Between Earth and Sky* [Bruchac, 1996], is signed by the illustrator. His name is Thomas Locker, and he actually signs his name so that it looks like a self-portrait. See his mustache and curly hair? What an artist!"

When they finish distributing the books, Bob says, "Please start by looking through the books on your desk. Then you can trade if you'd like. You can also look for other books in the crate. I'll put it in the back of the room near your library. You'll have time tomorrow morning to get together with one or two other students and decide which book you'd like to present to the class. Mr. Korth and I will be here to help you."

Students spend the next few minutes flipping through pages, talking together about their discoveries, and walking around the room to search for interesting picture books.

At the end of the session, a student who was near the world map comes up to Bob with a big smile on his face. "I put a pin on the Yucatán peninsula," he proclaims. "I'm reading *Tikal*. It's a great book."

What could be a better conclusion to the morning's work?

Fluency Through Picture Books

Day 2: *Wednesday (instructional time: 2 hours, 45 minutes)*

9:20–10:00—Library (selection of books; practice in small groups)

11:20–12:00—DEAR (free reading of multiple picture books; two presentations)

Apple Valley Alli (Stanley, 2006)
Confetti: Poems for Children (Mora, 1996)

12:50–1:35—ELA (practice in small groups/free reading; one presentation)

Uptown (Collier, 2000)

1:35–2:15—Social Studies (practice in small groups/free reading; five presentations)

Tikal (Mann, 2002)
Giving Thanks: A Native American Good Morning Message (Swamp, 1995)
Crazy Horse's Vision (Bruchac, 2000)
The Great Kapok Tree: A Tale of the Amazon Rain Forest (Cherry, 1990)
The Other Side (Woodson, 2001)

During the planning session that Mike and Bob had at a ping-pong table a few weeks before they facilitated this classroom activity, Mike said, "Choice is good." They were talking about how they could divide the class into groups and whether they should assign particular books to particular students using Mike's estimation of their reading abilities. They decided to allow the students to choose books based on their interest. Students could form their own working groups of two or three individuals with the goal of presenting a picture book to the rest of the class. Mike and Bob reasoned that it would be possible to ensure a high level of comfort, and that, since he knows the students so well, Mike could intervene if they had trouble working together effectively. If difficulties with the text were encountered, both educators would be there to help—much as Bob had done years ago as a school reading specialist. Instead of just working with children who were on his caseload, Bob would join his assigned teacher in assisting anyone who needed help, thereby reducing the teacher-student ratio to a manageable 1:12.

On the second day of the project, students select their books and their groups. For 30 minutes, the groups practice in small clusters throughout the room and in the hallway. Later, just before lunch, the DEAR ("drop everything and read") time gives people a chance to investigate books they had not chosen for their group presentations. Here are some of the comments Bob overhears:

"Look, mine has Spanish in it!"—leafing through Mora's poems.

"How funny: A flying cow."—pointing to an illustration in *Magellan's World* that shows livestock being loaded onto one of the explorers ships using ropes and pulleys (Waldman, 2007, p. 17).

"The author signed this one."—looking at the title page of Lynne Cherry's *The Armadillo from Amarillo* (1994).

"My book is by that same author."—pointing to the cover of *The Great Kapok Tree*.

Besides modeling DEAR by reading their own books, Mike and Bob are both keeping an eye on what's going on. Because this isn't SSR (sustained silent reading), the students may interact quietly, as long as the noise level doesn't disturb anyone. Bob notices that two boys are working on the book they chose for their presentation. He walks over to them, ready to suggest that they put the book away for now and read something else from the crate. As he gets close to their desks, they both look up and say, with great enthusiasm, "We're ready to read ours to the class!" Ah, yes, teaching is about knowing when to be flexible.

They have chosen *Apple Valley Alli,* a book that was locally written and published by Jan Stanley, a former seventh-grade English teacher from upstate New York. The book uses rhyming verse and is filled with photographs from a child's visit to an orchard. "Okay," Bob tells the boys, "let me hear you read a bit of the book." They do a very nice job, so he figures they are ready.

Bob is very happy to start with this locally relevant book and these two eager readers. He announces that there will be one presentation before lunch. Another group, the poetry readers from yesterday, ask if they can read this morning as well.

Both presentations are wonderful. After each, the students give the "Blue" cheer—a version of "Two, four, six, eight, who do we appreciate?" that Mike has instituted in the classroom to promote camaraderie. Then everyone heads for lunch.

Using Fluency to Focus on Comprehension

Over burgers, Mike and Bob discuss how things are going. They realize that they'll need to highlight the social studies topics addressed by the books. Mike's other preparation for the test includes doing practice questions first thing in the morning and discussing general concepts from the grades 1–4 curriculum. When Mike and Bob wonder about whether the students will benefit from switching back and forth among the many subjects presented by the assortment of picture books, they realize that standardized tests are also filled with a broad range of topics and that the questions jump from one thing to the next very quickly.

"Besides," Bob says, "what we're doing is similar to the main idea in *Hooray for Diffendoofer Day!* (Dr. Seuss & Prelutsky, 1998). We are helping students become confident in their abilities to *think*. That is one thing that will definitely help them when they take a test."

Back in the classroom, students spend the rest of the afternoon practicing in their small groups and presenting to their classmates. Mike and Bob draw attention to social studies concepts after the Blue cheers have been given. Pins are put on the map, and students who have finished their oral reading explore additional books.

Students—and their teachers—enjoy traveling through space and time. During the afternoon, they go to the streets of Harlem and the pyramids of the Yucatán. They discuss the natural wonders of Akwesasne and the troubled times of the American plains. They hear the animals of the Amazon and see the old fences of the segregated South. They do all of this without leaving the classroom or paying a cent. "I wonder why some people think picture books are only for toddlers," Bob muses.

Evidence of Success

Mike has decided to ask the children to write thank-you notes to Bob in the afternoon from the standpoint of characters from books that he has shared with them. "Put yourselves in the books," he tells them. "Have the books speak." All of the "Thank-You Books" Bob received a week later were full of colorful artwork. Crazy Horse looked just as he did during his vision quest. Many animals from Brazil voiced their thanks. A pop-up book from the orchard made a big, red apple jump forward when the cover was opened. Bob's portable book crate was carefully drawn by the book from the bayou. The Harlem book declared that the boys liked the part where the buildings were made of chocolate. The book of confetti spoke poetically, of course, and the message from Africa was clear:

> Thank you for letting us share our words and pictures with the class.
> Thank you for letting us stop the drought in Kapiti Plain. Thanks for
> taking us to Mr. Korth's classroom.

The detailed drawings and imaginative messages were created after Bob had taken the picture books out of the room. Everything was done from memory. That same feat of memory might have been a factor in the high degree of success that the students achieved in the social studies test a few weeks later. It's hard to say.

On a hot day in June, six months after the activity, Bob returned to Mike's classroom to talk with the students about picture books. He asked, "How can preparing to read out loud help you understand a difficult book?" Here are a few of the responses:

"It let you hear it for yourself instead of just hearing it in your mind."

"When we had to practice, it would kind of get in our mind to understand."

"We could make a connection between the print and the pictures."

Here's what students said when asked, "Can reading out loud make you a better reader?"

"Yes, because your friends will correct you when you say a word wrong."

"I can understand it easier—if the words are long, I can pronounce them out loud."

"You don't know you're making a mistake if you read silently."

Mike is certain that his students benefit from opportunities to read books to their peers. Why? Because it is one of the ways that learners participate in a joyful experience—fluently reading and actively constructing meaning—as they explore the wonderful literature provided by picture books.

Reflections

1. What are some ways to encourage students to model fluent reading for their classmates without appearing to be "showing off" their abilities?

2. What kinds of picture books will engage older students in meaningful reading activities?

3. Because picture books take time to appreciate, can instructional time be used to allow students to explore them at a leisurely pace?

4. How could teachers involve students and their families in visits to public libraries to find picture books for classroom bookshelves?

5. How might the logistics be worked out so that English and social studies units can be taught together by multiple teachers?

6. How would you implement an approach such as Mike Korth and Bob Ackland's over an entire year?

7. What characteristics in trade books lend themselves to reading for fluency?

8. How can collaboration between literacy professionals (e.g. Mike and Bob) enhance reading instruction for students?

Picture Books With Connections to Social Studies

Topics: **E** = Economics   **G** = Geography   **H** = History   **I** = Immigration

Aardema, Verna. (1981). *Bringing the rain to Kapiti Plain.* An African tale of persistence through a drought. **E, G**

Appelt, Kathi. (1995). *Bayou lullaby.* Bedtime story from Louisiana with a Cajun glossary. **G**

Armitage, Ronda, & Armitage, David. (1989). *The lighthouse keeper's rescue.* Adventure on the sea and land gives a sense of life on the Atlantic coast. **E, G**

Bruchac, Joseph. (1996). *Between Earth and sky: Legends of Native American sacred places.* Tales from many cultures help us understand the origin and importance of major landmarks. **G, H**

Bruchac, Joseph. (2000). *Crazy Horse's vision.* As settlers and soldiers moved into the western plains, a young man heads off on a vision quest. **G, H**

Buffett, Jimmy, & Buffett, Savannah Jane. (1988). *The Jolly Mon.* The Caribbean comes to life in this tale. **G**

Bunting, Eve. (2006). *One green apple.* A girl who is just starting to learn English and who wears a traditional dupatta (headscarf) goes on a field trip to an orchard. **G, I**

Burg, Ann E. (2003). *E is for empire: A New York State alphabet.* Books about other states are included in the series. **E, G, H**

Cheney, Lynne. (2003). *A is for Abigail: An almanac of amazing American women.* Ill. Robin Preiss Glasser. **E, H**

Cherry, Lynne. (1990). *The great kapok tree: A tale of the Amazon rain forest.* **E, G**

Cherry, Lynne. (1994). *The armadillo from Amarillo.* An armadillo sends postcards from all the wonderful places he visits in Texas and beyond. **G**

Coleman, Evelyn. (1996). *White socks only.* Segregation is confronted when a girl thinks that the "Whites Only" sign at a drinking fountain refers to the color of people's socks. **E, H**

Collier, Bryan. (2000). *Uptown.* A young man takes us on a collage-filled tour through the vibrant locales of Harlem. **E, G**

Grace, Catherine O'Neill, & Bruchac, Margaret M., with Plimoth Plantation. (2001). *1621: A new look at Thanksgiving.* This detailed account breaks many stereotypes. **E, G, H**

Harness, Cheryl. (2001). *Remember the ladies: 100 great American women.* **E, H**

Hoffman, Mary. (1995). *Boundless Grace: Sequel to* Amazing Grace. Grace visits her father and his new wife in Africa and keeps in mind that "Families are what you make them.' (p. 8). **G**

Kalman, Bobbie. (2001). *Life in a longhouse village.* **E, G, H**

Kalman, Maira. (2002). *Fireboat: The heroic adventures of the John J. Harvey.* The true story of a decommissioned fireboat that came to the aid of New York City on September 11, 2001. **G, H**

Kennedy, Edward M. (2006). *My senator and me: A dog's-eye view of Washington, D.C.* Ill. David Small. A day in the life of a United States senator. **E, H**

Lawlor, Veronica (Ed. & Ill.). (1995). *I was dreaming to come to America: Memories from the Ellis Island Oral History Project.* **E, G, H, I**

Lester, Julius. (2005). *Let's talk about race.* Lester presents a first-person narrative that will prompt meaningful discussion. **G, H**

Mann, Elizabeth. (2002). *Tikal.* Ill. Tom McNeely. The Mayan world prior to 900 A.D. comes to life in this thoroughly researched and richly illustrated text. **E, G, H**

Meuse-Dallien, Theresa. (2003). *The sharing circle: Stories about First Nations culture.* Ill. Arthur Stevens. Halifax, NS, Canada: Nimbus. Set in a 21st century community, this account of childhood demonstrates the connections between past and present. **G, H**

Mora, Pat. (1996). *Confetti: Poems for children.* Ill. Enrique O. Sanchez. Harmonies of Spanish and English herald the life, movement, and joy of the American southwest. **G, I**

Mora, Pat. (1997). *Tomás and the library lady.* Ill. Raul Colón. A son of a migrant farmworker family finds that books have stories he can share. Tomás Rivera became the chancellor of the University of California at Riverside. **E, G, H, I**

Nikola-Lisa, W. (1997). *Till year's good end: A calendar of medieval labors.* Ill. Christopher Manson. Medieval life moves through the seasons in this tale of laborers in Europe. **E, G, H**

Perez, Amanda Irma. (2002). *My diary from here to there. Mi diario de aqui hast alla.* Ill. Maya Christina Gonzalez. [Dual language: Spanish/English.] **E, G, I**

Polacco, Patricia. (1994). *Pink and Say.* A true story of friendship and sacrifice during the American Civil War. **H**

Ruurs, Margriet. (2005). *My librarian is a camel: How books are brought to children around the world.* Honesdale, PA: Boyds Mills Press. **E, G**

Stanley, Janice Dave. (2006). *Apple Valley Alli.* Ill. Tamia. Plattsburgh, NY: Author. **E, G**

Swamp, Jake. (1995). *Giving thanks: A Native American good morning message.* The author explains, "The words in this book are based on the Thanksgiving Address, an ancient message of peace and appreciation of Mother Earth and all her inhabitants." (p. 5). **E, G, H**

Waldman, Stuart. (2007). *Magellan's world.* Ill. Gregory Manchess. This detailed record of Ferdinand Magellan's voyage of discovery includes facsimile journal entries and vibrant artwork. **E, G, H**

Waters, Kate. (1989). *Sarah Morton's day: A day in the life of a Pilgrim girl.* Photos from Plimoth Plantation give us a sense of the life of a young colonist in the 1600s. **E, G, H**

Winter, Jeanette. (2004). *September roses.* This story of kindness and healing takes place in the days following September 11, 2001. **G, H**

Woodson, Jacqueline. (2001). *The other side.* Two girls decide whether they should cross the fence of segregation in the rural South in the mid-twentieth century. **E, G, H**

Yazzie, Evangeline Parsons. (2005). *Dzání Yázhi Naazbaá—Little Woman Warrior who came home: A story of the Navajo Long Walk.* [Dual language: Navajo/English.] **G, H**

Yolen, Jane. (1992). *Encounter.* Ill. David Shannon. The 1492 landing of Columbus is told from the point of view of a young Taino boy. **E, G, H**

Source: Robert T. Ackland (State University of New York, Plattsburgh)

Synergistic and
Systematic Fluency
Instruction in La Vista, Nebraska

Reading fluency can be fostered in a number of ways in the classroom. These include teacher-modeled fluent reading, which allows students to develop an internal sense of what it means to be fluent; assisted reading, during which students read a text and hear it read to them at the same time; repeated or rehearsed reading; performance of one's reading for an audience; and focused study of the words within a passage that has just been read. While all of these approaches are important in developing readers' fluency, combining them into a single-lesson format offers the potential to reap gains that are more than the sum of the parts. We call this notion of creating lessons that combine multiple aspects of fluency instruction a "synergistic approach."

One synergistic approach that has proven effective is the Fluency Development Lesson, or FDL (National Reading Panel, 2000a). The lesson is as follows:

✱ Students are assigned a short text for fluency instruction.

✱ The teacher reads the text to the students.

✱ The teacher then reads it with the students.

✱ Last, the students practice the passage on their own several times. This is followed by an opportunity for students to read the passage to an audience. A focused study of some key words from the passage completes the lesson.

Michelle Rezek is a teacher from La Vista, Nebraska, who made the FDL an integral part of the reading curriculum in her fifth-grade classroom. Even for older students, a systematic and synergistic approach to fluency instruction can be beneficial.

Fluency Instruction

For the past several years, Michelle Rezek has taught fifth grade at G. Stanley Hall Elementary School in La Vista, Nebraska. La Vista is a largely middle-class suburb of Omaha and has a large population of military families from the nearby Offutt Air Force

Base located in Bellevue. G. Stanley Hall is a Title I School, indicating that there is a substantial degree of poverty within the school's boundaries.

Over her years in the classroom, Michelle has noted that reading fluency seemed to be a major concern for many of her students who were experiencing significant difficulty in acquiring grade-level reading skills and proficiencies. She had many students who, while quite bright, often had difficulty reading the words on the page accurately and with ease and expression. Moreover, the basal reading program did not seem to provide the kinds of reading experiences that would lead to higher levels of fluency. "The basal was like dragging students through the Boston Marathon. They could do it, but there was little joy, enthusiasm, or meaning associated with their reading," explained Michelle.

So, after hearing professional development presentations on reading fluency, she decided to make fluency a priority in her classroom and to include it in her two-hour block of time devoted to reading and reading instruction. Poetry, songs, and short plays began to be regular parts of her reading curriculum. Shadow puppet shows on a bedsheet hanging from the ceiling was a particular favorite. Students also created overhead slide shows to supplement their performances—the slide shows showed the text of the poem or song or pictures that reflected the content of the passage. Although students had fun while performing their shows, they were also reading—reading and rereading with the purpose of conveying meaning to an audience. Students loved to perform their passages in front of their classmates, but Michelle found other ways for students to perform. They performed for her, for parents, for partners, for other classrooms. They even recorded passages on the classroom computers for later analysis by Michelle and to create a recorded portfolio of individual students' fluency development over the school year.

After providing students with scripts (Aaron Shepherd [aaronshep.com] was a favorite source), students began to write their own, based on trade books that they were reading in class and independently. Some of the first scripts were based on Arnold Lobel's award-winning *Fables*. These brief tales with a great deal of dialogue were ideal for transforming into scripts that students could then practice and perform for an audience. At first, the oral reading practice culminated in quarterly fluency celebrations. As students became more adept and enthusiastic in oral reading performance, the celebrations came more often. Eventually, students began to write their own scripts, poems, and other passages for performance from the books that they were reading in the guided reading portion of their curriculum.

Later, word study activities were added into her fluency instruction. After having practiced and performed a passage, students would be asked to engage in examining selected words from the passage. Words from fluency texts found their way onto word walls and into word activities that Michelle would devise for students. Word walls, word games, and idiom activities were among the students' favorites.

Michelle also made sure to read to her students regularly—to expose them to the best literature available and to model for students what expressive, enthusiastic, and meaningful reading sounds like. She began to hear other teachers tell their own students to "read like you were Mrs. Rezek!"

The Fluency Development Lesson

As time went on, Michelle noted that even more intensive fluency and word study was called for. And so, she began to experiment with the Fluency Development Lesson (See page 53). The FDL is a specific lesson format for students experiencing difficulty in reading. Each lesson contains a strong focus on students engaged in repeated readings of authentic texts meant to be read with expression and meaning—simple poetry comes first and was followed by dialogues, scripts, and then poems that contains written features such as voice, rhyme, dialect, alliteration, and assonance.

The FDL is a 10- to 15-minute daily fluency activity in which students are given a text that they work on for fluency. The lesson begins with the teacher reading the passage several times to students as the students follow along silently on their own copy of the passage. The teacher models fluent reading during this read-aloud. Students and teacher then chat a bit about the content of the text and about how the teacher helped to make meaning with her voice. After modeling the reading, the students and teachers read the text chorally several times. Next, students practice the passage with the partner, one student reading to another several times and the partner following along, giving feedback and helping out when necessary. Roles are then reversed after two or three readings. Students rate themselves and their partners using a simple Fluency Rubric that is posted in the room. With so much practice, students are then invited to perform their passage for an audience—classmates, other classrooms, or teachers, parents, the principal, or anyone willing to listen to a student performance and give specific praise for the reading. Students can read solo or in duets, trios, quartets, or larger groups. A brief word study activity usually follows the students' performance, with the words chosen by the teacher and students from the passage that is rehearsed. The words go on the word wall and in students' word banks (individual notebooks or decks of index cards that contain the words) and are then analyzed, sorted, practiced, and used in word games. Students are also encouraged to use the words in their own oral and written language.

Michelle employed FDL with her students two to three times per week. The brevity of the lessons meant that she could implement it whenever she had a few minutes— first thing in the morning, right after lunch, near the end of the day. Moreover, because the genre or topic of the material used in the text could vary, she used texts that could be integrated into social studies, science, art, music, or any other subject area.

Michelle has found other ways to focus on fluency in her classroom. She has expanded her use of FDL with fluency notebooks. Each student has a fluency notebook that contains a letter explaining the importance of fluency and icons that represent the key fluency traits. At the end of a lesson, the FDL passage is pasted in the notebook. The notebooks are sent home with students for further practice. Students accumulate as many signatures as possible in their notebooks from "lucky listeners" at home or in their neighborhood who listen to them read their passage. "Lucky listeners" can even be found at school (parent volunteers, para-professionals, literacy coaches, other teachers, school staff, etc.).

Michelle also finds meaty sentences or quotes from content texts the students will be reading for the day's lesson. She types these sentences on cards and passes them out to her

The Fluency Development Lesson (FDL): Synergistic Instruction

The FDL (Rasinski, 2010) employs relatively short reading passages (poems, rhymes, songs, story segments, or other texts) that students read and reread over a short period of time. The format for the lesson follows a routine of the teacher taking responsibility for reading the daily passage and gradually shifting responsibility for the reading to the students.

1. The teacher introduces a new short text and reads it to the students two or three times while the students follow along silently. The text can be a poem, segment from a basal passage or trade book selection, etc.

2. The teacher and students discuss the nature and content of the passage as well as the quality of the teacher's reading of the passage.

3. Teacher and students read the passage chorally several times. Antiphonal choral reading (Rasinski, 2010) and other variations are used to create variety and maintain engagement.

4. The teacher organizes students into pairs or trios. Each student practices the passage three times while his or her partner listens and provides support and encouragement.

5. Individuals and groups of students perform their reading for the class or other audience such as another class, a parent visitor, the school principal, or another teacher.

6. The students and their teacher then choose four to five interesting words from the text to add to individual students' word banks and/or the classroom word wall.

7. Students engage in 5–10 minutes of word study activities (e.g., word sorts with word bank words, word walls, flash card practice, defining words, word games, etc.).

8. Students take a copy of the passage home to practice with parents and other family members.

9. The following day, students read the passage from the previous day chorally to the teacher or a fellow student for accuracy and fluency. Words from the previous day are also read, reread, grouped, and sorted by students and groups of students. Students may also read the passage to the teacher or a partner who checks for fluency and accuracy.

The instructional routine then begins again with step 1, using a new passage.

Source: Rasinski, T. V. (2010). *The fluent reader: Oral reading strategies for building word recognition, fluency, and comprehension* (2nd ed.). New York: Scholastic.

A **Close-Up** Look Into **15 Diverse Classrooms**

students. The students rehearse their assigned sentence until they can read it fluently. She then has the students share their sentences orally with other classmates. After students have performed their individual sentences, she asks students to predict the content of the day's reading. Michelle explains that this has been a fabulous way to integrate fluency with comprehension and content area reading: "After the sharing of sentences, students are ready to dive into reading the entire text."

Evidence of Success

Michelle notes that the emphasis on fluency, especially the Fluency Development Lesson, has a positive impact on her students' overall reading development. Calvin is a case in point. Calvin began the year in Michelle's class as an exceptionally poor reader. He not only read poorly; he had come to believe that he was unable to become a good reader. His body language told it all. When reading orally, he read in a slow, monotonous voice (he began fifth grade reading at the second-grade level [fewer than 60 words per minute]), making many word recognition errors, and didn't understand much of what he read. Moreover, he usually slumped while reading, made little eye contact, and spoke so softly that his voice could barely be heard by someone sitting less than three feet away. Calvin had largely given up on himself as a reader and a learner.

Michelle used fifth grade to focus on fluency with Calvin and other students experiencing difficulty in reading. They practiced and performed passages often throughout the school year, they engaged in paired reading (Rasinski, 2010) with a para-professional and other students, and they worked with the FDL regularly. Calvin engaged in a daily, 10-minute paired reading activity with a teacher's aide, during which he and the aide read a passage together simultaneously and aloud. The aide supported Calvin with her own voice, helping him get through challenging parts of a passage and being a cheerleader for his reading efforts. Calvin's mother began to notice a difference in his reading, and she began to do paired reading at home with him on a regular basis. Michelle charted Calvin's (and other students') growth in fluency by regularly observing Calvin read and recording her observations on the Fluency Notes and Observations chart (see page 56). She could show Calvin how his reading had improved over the school year.

By the end of the year, Calvin was reading at grade level, for comprehension as well as fluency, according to the Metropolitan Achievement Test and other measures of reading proficiency. He was able to read grade-level texts at 130 words correct per minute, with few errors and excellent comprehension. The highlight of the year was when Calvin read at a school board meeting. He received an ovation, a response that Michelle is certain he will remember for all his life.

Calvin was certainly one success story, but he was by no means the only one. Michelle reports that fluency instruction, especially her use of FDL, has had a tremendous impact on her struggling readers. She states that reading fluency seems to be the issue that holds many of these students back. "These are clearly smart kids who have a lot going for them, but this lack of fluency had made it difficult to enjoy and appreciate the stories that they read and learn from the texts that are assigned. They spin their wheels trying to read and understand the words; they hardly ever get to the point of making sense of the entire passage." Struggling readers in Michelle's class demonstrate greater improvements in reading than what was found in other classrooms and schools in the district. Moreover, even the good readers seemed to enjoy the FDL and other fluency activities, as they gave these students the opportunity to explore how words and texts could be interpreted in various ways with the voice.

Perhaps the greatest impact and evidence of the power of Michelle's work in fluency could be found when her work began to snowball. Other teachers in her school and around the district began to make reading fluency a priority in their classrooms. Michelle Rezek now works as a literacy coach and facilitator at Hickory Hill Elementary School in nearby Papillion. Although she no longer has a classroom she can call her own, she reports that she now has the opportunity to affect many classrooms and many children.

Reflections

1. What are the benefits of a systematic and synergistic approach to fluency instruction such as the FDL?

2. How might you alter or modify the FDL to fit your own classroom? Is there anything you might add or delete from the lesson?

3. Systematic approaches to fluency instruction need to follow a predictable routine so that students know it is an integral part of the curriculum and they have a good understanding of how the lesson is implemented. In your own teaching, think about how you might make a lesson such as the FDL a routine part of your instruction. What time of day would be best to implement it? What arrangements would you have to make in your classroom for it work?

4. How might you involve parents in your own systematic and synergistic fluency instruction?

5. How would you measure student progress and the overall success of a systematic and synergistic approach to fluency in your own classroom?

Fluency Notes and Observations

The teacher records her or his observations of individual students' oral reading fluency. Done on a regular basis (e.g., once a month), it will provide teachers with a record of students' growth in reading fluency as well indicators of specific areas of strength and concern in students' reading.

Student Name: _____   Date: _____

Passage Read: _____

Overall Fluency			
Expression			
Phrasing			
Smoothness			
Pace	Fast Slow Just Right		Rate

Rainbow Reading
in Nelson, New Zealand

Most of us learned the motto "Practice makes perfect" as we were growing up. We know from playing sports, studying musical instruments, and even learning how to tie slip knots in Scout camp that the more we practice, the better we get. The same motto holds true in learning to read. When children practice rereading a text, it has been shown that they make impressive reading gains (Samuels, 1979). Practicing doesn't work, however, if we don't know what a good performance looks like. We need to see experts playing the sport we're trying to learn in order to see how it looks in action. We need to hear beautiful music so that we can tell when our own playing sounds more like it. We need to see a perfect slip knot to imitate it. When children are learning to read, hearing a proficient reader read the book as they read along has a similar effect. Audio-assisted reading gives a model that helps provide support as children learn to read aloud and silently (Carbo, 1978a; Chomsky, 1976). It has been found that striving readers who read a text while simultaneously listening to a recording of it make gains in word recognition, fluency, and comprehension (Carbo, 1978b, 1981; Kuhn & Stahl, 2000; Smith & Elley, 1997). Listening while reading also helps move students away from a teacher-centered classroom to a classroom that encourages independent practice.

Audio-Assisted Fluency

As a resource reading teacher, Meryl-Lynn Pluck was expected to regularly make the rounds to visit 85 at-risk students, spanning a number of grade levels, in 19 schools in Nelson, New Zealand. Feeling overwhelmed by the caseload and having nightmares about "illiterate, delinquent, suicidal teenagers" (Pluck, 2006, p. 193) should she fail in her task, she struggled to come up with a manageable but effective reading intervention that could be easily implemented by paraprofessionals working with students within all those schools. Well read in the research literature, fully trained in Reading Recovery, and with a master's degree specializing in reading difficulties supervised by Marie Clay, she took particular note of three articles written in the 1970s that highlighted the improvements striving readers experienced through repeated reading, especially with audio support.

A Close-Up Look Into 15 Diverse Classrooms

The year was 1993, and since fluency had not come onto the radar screen in the reading field at that time, there was no audio-assisted repeated reading program. Meryl-Lynn did what any enterprising—and desperate—teacher would do: She created one! Operating mostly on well-trained instinct, she selected 130 short, high-interest stories from the New Zealand's *School Journal*, enlisted "volunteers" to read them with good pace and expression onto audiotapes, and then recruited students within and outside her assigned caseload for a pilot study. The reading materials fell into seven levels, just enough to match the colors of the rainbow—and thus, Rainbow Reading was born.

She required all participating schools to agree to offer the program half an hour a day, five days a week, and to allow a student to remain in it until he or she reached grade level in reading; to allow students to leave class for the program, under the guidance of a teacher or aide; and to furnish each student with the books, a tape recorder, batteries, and a battery charger so they could listen to and read the stories outside of class.

After Meryl-Lynn created a short training manual for Rainbow Reading paraprofessionals and produced a video demonstration of the training, the program was launched.

The Reading Rainbow Program

In schools and districts where the Reading Rainbow program has been adopted, it is used throughout the academic year as part of the literacy instruction. All of the Rainbow Reading materials, regardless of their level or topic, contain a set of leveled texts, an audio CD to accompany each one, and instructions on how to use repeated oral reading as the core of the unit. An outline of a typical lesson follows:

* Working in a grouping of four to six, students are individually oriented to a story at their instructional reading level.

* Students listen to the stories on CD (or MP3 player) while reading them silently.

* After sufficient practice listening, they read them to a reading assistant.

* When students can read expressively, with at least 95% accuracy, and can demonstrate understanding of a story, they are allowed to move on to the next story.

* When they can read a new, unpracticed story at their level easily and with good comprehension, they move up to the next level.

* As students progress through the books, they keep track of their own progress by writing the names of each story read and the number of times they practiced it in a log.

* The log is shared with the reading assistant in conferences, and he or she adds positive comments about the reading experience in the margins.

* The program also includes fun, educational, text-related practice activities such as word games, cloze activities, writing exercises, and board games.

Evidence of Success

When data from her program was first evaluated, Meryl-Lynn couldn't have been prepared for the dramatic results. In the initial year, students gained an average of 2.2 years in their reading grade level—with some attaining four years of progress—from only 28 weeks on average in the program! The rapid progress in reading skills occurred across the grade levels, and included low-progress readers, as well as English language learners. Impressive gains were made in word recognition, oral language, reading accuracy, spelling, and reading comprehension. What's more, the kids loved it. Teachers stressed that students did not want to stop reading when the time was up. The progress in reading continued even after the intervention, and not surprisingly, those who read the most improved the most (Pluck, 2006).

How Rainbow Reading Grew Big

Fast-forward to the current time, and we find that the good word has gotten out. Meryl-Lynn left her teaching position to become a publisher, and Rainbow Reading has become a worldwide phenomenon.

How did Rainbow Reading grow so much? Meryl-Lynn notes that, like the character in the tale "The Shoemaker and the Elves," she has continually added to her offerings: new titles, levels, and activities whenever resources permitted. At the same time, she refreshes dated-looking stories and has transitioned from cassette tapes to CDs that have MP3 files. She mentions that CDs offer the ability to jump right to the target spot without spooling through tape. Most of all, however, Meryl-Lynn's programs have grown because she is a good listener when educators express their needs and share classroom feedback. For example, she recounts, "When a new, easier level was requested, we obliged, and it quickly became our best seller."

Meryl-Lynn's pioneering work found fertile ground in another, unexpected setting: "When a version was requested in the Maori language, I willingly agreed to be the consultant and gave permission for the Rainbow Reading model to be used. 'Te Huinga Raukura,' available in four levels to date, is now freely available to all schools teaching Maori, funded by the New Zealand Ministry of Education." As a result, Rainbow Reading is not only international but multilingual.

Recently, Meryl-Lynn created Speak Out, a series of multilevel scripts for Readers Theater projects, accompanied by a recording of each script on CD. She is also co-developer of CSI—Comprehension Strategies Instruction. CSI employs a gradual-release model, from teacher modeling to cooperative learning and independent reflection. In CSI, students in grade 3 and beyond apply several reading comprehension strategies to content across language arts, math, science, and social studies. The program consists of interactive, whiteboard-enabled digital texts for use in shared reading, audio-assisted hard-copy texts for cooperative learning, and an independent reflection journal for each student.

Meryl-Lynn has also addressed the reading needs of reluctant boy readers with a series called Toxic, high-interest stories that involve "animals (and humans) with horrifying

Benefits of Audio-Assisted Reading

Benefit	Factor
Good modeling of fluent reading	Book is read fluently but slowly enough for student to read along. Reading gets faster as books get more difficult.
Students make rapid progress	Each student engages in just the right amount of practice they require as an individual so that accelerated progress occurs. Student works at best pace for him or her, on own book and at own level.
Reading is achievable	Books are leveled; student reads books at instructional reading level. Books have a gradual gradient of difficulty. Student is set up to succeed during orientation.
Students experience success	Students practice each book until they can read it accurately, fluently, and with good understanding.
Students are motivated to read	Books are of high interest to students whose interest levels exceed their reading levels, and are presented in an interesting manner. Students are supported.
Students read a variety of quality material	Books by a selection of good authors on a variety of topics and genres prepare students for reading anything and everything.
Increase in reading "mileage"	Students' books are short and appealing enough to interest students in rereading.
Concentration on comprehension	All activities involve reading meaningful text. Comprehension is facilitated and taught during orientation and it is checked during conference.
Vocabulary extension	Opportunities to extend vocabulary during orientation and conference are many. Books have glossaries. Activities extend vocabulary.
Opportunities to practice a variety of types of reading in a variety of settings	There are many opportunities to practice reading at both an easy and instructional level, with and without support, alone and to an audience. Text-related activities provide opportunities for reading in a different format and/or applying learning to a new situation.
Useful feedback	Students receive useful feedback on strategies and progress during regular conferences with teacher.
Students self-monitor, control and take responsibility for their learning	Students are encouraged to make decisions about their program (decide on next steps) and to self-monitor their program and progress by keeping a brief record of practices.

Source: Meryl-Lynn Pluck, author of the Rainbow Reading Program, New Heights, Speak Out! Readers' Theater, and CSI—Comprehension Strategies Instruction; www.rainbowreading.co.nz

habits, stinky creatures, and animal cannibals," she shudders, among other boy-favored topics. She has young males record audio versions of the stories, and each tale has optional reading-related activities, including a "Make and Do" activity, which gets students reading and following instructions.

Meryl-Lynn is currently developing a series of books with audio support and related activities to address the needs of struggling adult readers who are age 14 and older but have reading abilities as low as the first- or second-grade level.

These grand programs, born of midnight fretting, are now making a global contribution to reading practice.

Reflections

1. Meryl-Lynn's background was in Reading Recovery. Based on your knowledge of Reading Recovery and the brief description in this chapter, which aspects of the fluency instruction seem similar? Which aspects seem different?

2. Do you think there are differences between reading fiction aloud versus reading nonfiction aloud? Could Readers Theater easily be performed with nonfiction texts? What about poetry or other genres? Discuss.

3. Think of a classroom setting with which you are familiar. What aspects of that literacy program include components of fluency?

4. Meryl-Lynn's Toxic series was designed especially for boys. Have you noticed some favorite authors or books that are very popular with boys? Which books tend to be very popular with girls? Which books have you found to be equally popular with both genders?

5. If you were developing recorded materials for your own classroom, what texts would you choose to record first? Whom would you choose to read them?

6. Think about people you know at home and at work who have certain vocal qualities that would work well with characters in texts. Are certain people or voices a "natural" for reading some of the classic fairy tales you know?

Guided Oral Reading

With Informational Text
in Burlington, Vermont

David Liben, a middle-school teacher mentor in Burlington, reflected on his work in helping teachers address some of the challenges they face while encouraging young adolescents to develop literacy skills and strategies.

"When students say, 'I can't read,' they are often thinking, 'I am stupid,'" David told me. "In my experience, these kids who are struggling the most have a fluency problem. We can tell them they're not stupid, but they know teachers are supposed to say this. Instead, we can break reading down into its elements as suggested by the National Reading Panel (NICHD, 2000a, 200b). We can say, 'Let's work on your fluency, so reading will not be so hard for you.' Then we have a chance of convincing them," he says. "If we follow this up by telling them they can become more fluent the same way they get better at layups, or fixing cars—by practice—they are even more likely to accept what we are saying. If we then provide the opportunity to practice and show them the positive results, we can truly 'seal the deal' and change their attitude toward reading."

"It's a confidence issue," David continues. "By the time struggling readers get to high school, this attitude about their abilities is really hard to change. In many cases, they have been failing with reading since first grade. We can give them activities that point out the progress they are making in fluency," he says, "and we can help them develop connections between fluency and comprehension. We can do differentiated instruction in our classrooms so that individuals get the kinds of support they need and so that they can see their own improvement."

"Here is the beauty of concentrating on oral reading fluency with struggling readers: They can tell when they are getting better at it. Students sometimes have a general idea that reading is becoming a bit easier—that they are able to understand more difficult text. But that can be very abstract. Their growth as readers through oral reading is much more apparent."

Fluency Assessment

David indicates that many schools in Vermont are using Timothy Rasinski and Nancy Padak's 3-Minute Reading Assessments (2005d). He's also seen educators take advantage of online versions of fluency assessments at the high school level (Ohio Literacy Alliance, 2007). Pre- and post-screenings can allow students to become consciously aware of their reading rate and can prompt them to set their sights on increasing the number of words they read accurately in a given passage. Teachers or paraprofessionals administer the three-minute assessments to everyone early in the year. After a given amount of time (sometimes a few weeks, sometimes more), readers who had trouble with fluency during the first assessment are assessed again. The students themselves can chart their progress on instruments such as the "Word Recognition Error Analysis Form" (Rasinski, 2004a, p. 168) and take more ownership in their development as readers.

But David sounds a note of caution about students assessing themselves. "A number of teachers have told me that students sometimes get the idea that reading faster is the entire goal," he says. "They focus on increasing their 'words correct per minute' score as an end in itself, so they have a tendency to drop the prosody in a passage. When teachers become aware of this, they need to step in and help students bring attention to the meaning of the text." One way to do this is to encourage students to "chunk" a passage into phrases as they read. As Rasinski points out, "This is important because often meaning lies in a text's phrases and not in its individual words.... Fluent readers are able to decode well and chunk a text in ways that make its meaning more accessible" (2004a, p. 32).

Teaching Practices

In conjunction with fluency assessments, teachers can create content-based questions, use reciprocal teaching (Palincsar & Brown, 1984) or reciprocal teaching "plus" (Ash, 2002) and integrate QAR (question-answer relationship) activities into their classroom instruction (Rafael, 1986) so that students make connections between fluency and comprehension. (For descriptions of these and many other meaning-oriented instructional practices, consult Ash & Kuhn, 2006.)

Structured Journals

An activity that David calls "structured journals" is an additional method for giving students the responsibility to monitor the advances they make in literacy, particularly with expository text. David places the description of this approach in an important context. "We have to keep in mind that good teaching should be an art that is based on a science," he says. "Here's an example of the science: 'Students who make predictions and summaries *as they read*, who monitor their own understanding, and who reflect on the implications of an author's intentions are able to get a great deal of information and satisfaction from reading.' That's the science. The art is the way a teacher integrates it into instruction. There's nearly an infinite number of ways."

With this artistic variability in mind, David explains that teachers use many formats for structured journals, but the goal is to prompt students to interact with text as they read.

Some teachers ask learners to write on sticky notes; others use bound journals or loose-leaf notebooks. Students generate four types of questions/comments:

1. Clarifying Questions: "I'm confused. I know the author wants me to get something from this, but I'm not sure what it is."

2. Summaries: "This is the sense that I've made from this part of the text; these are the most important ideas."

3. "I Wonder" Questions: "I wonder why… how… if…."

4. Connections: "Here is how this relates to my life, to something else I read, or to events that are happening in the world around me."

David gives an example: "A girl in a 10th- or 11th-grade history class who was reading about the Spanish-American War wrote this 'I wonder' question in her structured journal: 'If women had been able to vote in the 19th century and men could not, I wonder if a lot of the history that we are reading would be different.' We may ask," David muses, "if this structured journal activity is connected to reading fluency. Well, fluency helps open the door to thoughtful, in-depth reading—so yes, it is connected."

The Fluency Packet

A themed issue of *Educational Leadership*, "What Research Says About Reading," included an article by David and his wife, Meredith Liben. The article, which describes Family Academy, the public school the two of them established in Harlem in 1991, talks about the years-long evolution of an effective reading program across grade levels. Teachers at Family Academy provided models of fluency during classroom read-alouds where "books and authors are a constant source of celebration and excitement" (Liben & Liben, 2004, p. 60). As a wonderful example of how research can be used to inform instruction in a manner that unleashes creativity, David and Meredith developed a "fluency packet" approach:

What the research on fluency revealed to us was simple: Reading text repeatedly increases fluency. Children love poems, riddles, and silly stories, so we made our students a 'fluency packet' filled with all kinds of short literature. Studying one selection each week, students read aloud at home daily and in front of the class at least once a week. A favorite of teachers and students alike, the fluency packet quickly became a springboard for a variety of writing and dramatic activities. (p. 60)

The General Knowledge Curriculum

"At Family Academy," David explained in a recent article, "we found fluency was an essential bridge from early to later reading. Fluency did not guarantee comprehension, but lack of fluency guaranteed a lack of comprehension, especially as students got older and text progressively more demanding" (Liben, 2008, p. 1).

To help children make sense of this more difficult text, David and Meredith developed a "General Knowledge Curriculum" (GKC) for science and social studies. The curriculum is described in an article in *Phi Delta Kappan* (Liben & Liben, 2005). To provide students with the background knowledge they so desperately need, "our primary goal was to create a program that facilitated children's thinking and reading ability simultaneously" (p. 402). The GKC includes a "word awareness" component that draws students' attention to "descriptive vocabulary, academic vocabulary, and literary vocabulary" so that they can keep track of their comprehension (p. 406). Because good readers self-question and self-check, the GKC also draws students' attention to the role that questions play in reading. By doing this, it helps them interpret the questions that are asked in testing situations:

> While standardized tests have often been used against schools and schoolchildren, they have only rarely been used to the students' advantage. It is time to turn that upside down. We had already learned that there is deep value in deconstructing the questions test-makers ask of test-takers. Doing so can enable readers to access their own understanding. Reading comprehension tests demand that children do their comprehending fast and well. After all, the standard reading test has 50 questions, almost all inferential. Of these 50 questions, at least 15 to 20 different question types [such as main idea, detail, or sequence of events] are likely to be represented (p. 404).

"Frontloading With Fluency"

Teachers in the intermediate grades, and in middle or high school, do their best to meet the needs of students who have a broad range of reading abilities. They often hear suggestions at professional development workshops that they should try to find instructional materials that cover the content at varying levels of difficulty. However, especially for subject-area teachers, this task is impractical, if not impossible. In response, some teachers go so far as to find articles on the Internet related to an instructional unit and rewrite them in a simplified format for their struggling readers. Other approaches include one-on-one instruction by a paraprofessional aide, small groups working with the teacher, or listening to audio versions of printed material that have been downloaded on MP3 players.

David has developed an approach that allows teachers to use the same informational text with the entire class: Frontloading With Fluency. It is a pre-reading activity that includes an introduction of domain and non-domain vocabulary, along with guided oral reading of portions of the text (see the steps on p. 66). Frontloading With Fluency can be used with textbooks or with expository materials from other sources.

Let's say, for instance, the class is studying climate change as part of a unit on ponds and ecosystems. The teacher goes to the school or public library and logs on to the InfoTrac system. InfoTrac is a national database of periodicals, including those for young

Frontloading With Fluency

Here's David Liben's approach for exploring informational text:

1. Read aloud the article's title, headings, and illustration captions with students.

2. Ask: What is this text about? Generate hypotheses at various times during the steps above. (What is this text about?)

3. Use guided oral reading to read the first paragraph and last paragraph aloud with the class.

4. Introduce vocabulary (domain, non-domain, and background)

5. Continue to make predictions and refine.

learners, such as *Scholastic News, Super Science, National Geographic Kids*, and *Weekly Reader*. The database can search for materials by grade level and subject. You can print full-text articles. Some schools purchase subscriptions to high-interest, student-oriented magazines and use them regularly for literacy activities with informational text. The print versions are filled with color photographs and excellent illustrations to accompany the articles.

Frontloading With Fluency can encourage all students, regardless of their reading ability, to participate in a discussion before trying to read the text on their own. The objective is to help learners activate their background knowledge and develop a hypothesis regarding the content and purpose of the text. Magazine articles, chapters in textbooks, or segments of informational books are especially suitable for this approach.

The Lesson Plan

The order in which to use the components of Frontloading With Fluency is dependent upon instructional need. For instance, some teachers choose to introduce vocabulary on the day before distributing the text. Professional decisions are made within the context of particular situations. As David reminds us, "Good teaching is an art based on a science."

It is not always necessary to read informational text from beginning to end. In a whole class setting in which all students have a copy of the article about alligators, the teacher directs students to examine the title, headings, and illustrations. Attention is then directed to the first page. Students follow along silently as the teacher or a student volunteer reads the first paragraph. This model of oral fluency allows students to literally "hear" the way the text can sound internally as they read it to themselves later.

After a discussion about the meaning of the first paragraph and an initial round of hypotheses comes the introduction of vocabulary that is vital to the understanding of the text. David has found that the concept of "tiered" vocabulary (Beck, McKeown & Kucan, 2002) can be very helpful to teachers. Beyond the tier-one, basic, high-frequency words that we often encounter, there are tier-three domain words that are relevant to a particular subject. As teachers, we can easily identify domain words such as *legislature* or *manifest destiny*, *radius* or *perimeter*, *ecosystem* or *niche*. Instructional materials often introduce new domain words with bold print or glossaries. It is important for teachers to help students to both understand and pronounce these words so that fluent reading will not be interrupted by stumbling over words that may not be in a student's listening or speaking lexicon (there's a domain word for you).

There is a tier of vocabulary that we often neglect: these tier-two words could be called non-domain words. Here are a few to consider: *variable*, *often*, *several*, *insidious*, *cooperative*, *elegant*, *multifaceted*. David once spoke with a science teacher who taught a whole session before he realized, to his amazement, that many of his students didn't know what he meant when he used the word "indent." If we discuss the meanings and contextual uses of non-domain words that teachers or students have identified, we can help the learning process to become more transparent. Following the logic of the amusing picture book *The Math Curse* (Scieszka, 1995), in which a student discovers that everything in the world could be viewed in terms of a math problem, we can help our students realize that all of us, young and old, are perpetually encountering new words as lifelong learners.

The Frontloading With Fluency process often concludes with a fluent oral reading of the last paragraph or summary section followed by a refining of the hypotheses that students have offered about the purpose and main ideas of the text. Students then read the article individually or in pairs, silently or orally.

Great Online Sources for Informational Text

Chicago History Museum
chicagohs.org

The Exploratorium
exploratorium.edu

General OneFile
gale.cengage.com/onefile

Library of Congress
loc.gov/families

National Geographic Kids
kids.nationalgeographic.com

Plimoth Plantation
plimoth.org

Scholastic News
scholastic.com

Verizon Thinkfinity
thinkfinity.org

Evidence of Success

Frontloading With Fluency places students of various reading abilities on a more level playing field, because they have all had an opportunity to explore the meaning of the text. David has even found that this approach is useful in situations where capable readers encounter difficult material. For instance, an AP Biology teacher told David that this approach had "dramatically enhanced her students' ability to understand their college-level textbooks." She was confident that all of her students could read the same instructional material. It provided a common ground for the entire class as well as a springboard for additional pursuits.

This leads, according to David, to a situation where students can peel off from a reliance on teacher-directed instruction. Depending on the complexity of a particular piece of content-area material, students will need varying degrees of support after Frontloading With Fluency has been used to introduce the text. Those students who need minimal assistance due to their background knowledge of the topic or their proficiency with skills and strategies can start to work independently. This leaves more time for the teacher to give help to the students who will benefit from a higher degree of assistance.

Once the students are familiar with the components of this strategy, they are often able to explore new content-area material on their own. Frontloading With Fluency can also prepare students to read aloud to their peers. By practicing the pronunciation of challenging vocabulary and complex sentence structures, by trying to understand the author's logic in presenting ideas in a particular order, and by directing conscious attention to comprehension, students can begin to see (and hear) themselves as readers. They can demonstrate how prosody helps to communicate meaning.

What will motivate struggling students to work on their fluency? Success. Evidence of success can be collected through brief, frequent assessments to help individuals determine that they are intelligent, capable readers. Real success, not hollow praise, will be the motivator. As David pointed out to me during breakfast at a diner way back in October of 2007, "It's not only that students find a subject engaging. The second part is that you are more motivated if it's a task you perceive you can succeed at. Middle school students who are given third-grade material can recognize that it is third grade material—we need to help them change perceptions so they conceive of themselves as readers."

Reflections

1. How can teachers convince colleagues and administrators that subject-area class time needs to be devoted to improving reading skills and strategies?

2. What are some sources for brief assessments of fluency that can be administered in ways that will not reduce instructional time?

3. What particular challenges have teachers encountered when students begin to move from narrative to expository text?

4. Can teachers in grades 4 and up have an influence on the amount of expository text that is used in the primary grades to prepare students for this type of text?

5. As David Liben says, "Good teaching is an art based on a science." What professional development activities can teachers design to share approaches they have found effective?

A Businessman Turned Fluency Teacher *and Researcher in Shelby County, Tennessee*

Every teacher faces practical problems in the classroom that seem to be resistant to the theoretical solutions he or she learned in college. "Action research" is a way for teachers to systematically study those everyday problems so they can improve their practice.

Although there is no one right way of doing action research, the following steps are usually part of the process.

* Identify the research question. As you think about your classroom, what are the things that keep you awake at night? Turn those nagging thoughts into a concise question.

* Decide what evidence you can collect to help you answer the question. Evidence might include observations, student self-assessments, test data, questionnaires, student work samples, interviews, etc.

* Decide when and how you will collect the evidence.

* Analyze the evidence you have collected by looking for patterns, or themes.

* Draw conclusions.

* Develop a plan for acting on what you've learned.

* Share what you have learned with others. Sharing can be as informal as conversations with your colleagues or as formal as presentations or professional articles.

A Close-Up Look Into **15 Diverse Classrooms**

A New Career

David Paige was a successful businessman. His career in sales and marketing had served him well for 20 years. "But I was getting tired of making the 90-day budget," he says. "I was getting bored. I kept reading these articles about schools and I decided teaching was what I really wanted to do." David took a 50 percent pay cut and followed his heart. Not only is he happy with his decision, but his students are benefiting tremendously and he is contributing to a growing body of research on fluency instruction.

Getting Started With Fluency

Even though David had worked in very demanding jobs throughout his business career, he told us that his first year of teaching in Shelby County, Tennessee, was the hardest job he'd ever had. For the first three months, he was completely exhausted by the end of the school day. He reflects:

> What was different was that during this first year I was continually working to find what worked for me as a teacher. This task was exhausting, but it was even more stimulating. I was forced to push myself and repeatedly step out of my comfort zone to figure out how best to reach my students. Somewhere around March of my first year, everything started to come together. My second year as a teacher was completely different, as I had passed much of the learning curve and could now focus on long-term improvements and deeper strategic knowledge and applications.

David has been teaching language arts and math for five years in a self-contained special education class for sixth graders. His classroom is fairly homogenous in terms of race: About 93 percent of the students are African American. In terms of learning needs and home backgrounds, the group is very diverse. A typical class will range from foster children who have been in many different schools to middle-class students who just don't read well. As a new teacher, he quickly realized a dilemma that has haunted special education for decades—many struggling learners may not actually be special education students. David writes:

> Half of my students should not be in this class. They got behind early on and have never caught up. In first grade, there's this slow, laborious reading. And now in fourth grade, they're still slow, laborious readers. Then, they start using aberrant strategies to hide the fact that they aren't as good a reader as the one next to them. I believe if they'd just gotten the fluency instruction they needed in first and second grades, they would be better readers and they wouldn't be here. When we do fluency work, many students make fast progress. At the same time, there's the other group that I know really does need special education services. They benefit from

fluency instruction also but they are just different readers with greater challenges due to their disabilities.

When David began using fluency strategies such as choral and repeated reading, he saw dramatic improvements in all of his students' reading. He was working on his master's degree at the time and decided that writing his thesis on fluency would help him better understand what was happening with fluency and his special education students.

Action Research Study: Reading Level

Most students in David's class were reading at about a third- to fourth-grade level. He decided to study the effects of repeated reading using fifth-grade-level texts. "They just seemed to flounder forever and ever in a third-grade text, so I wanted to see what would happen if they read more challenging text," he explains. Lois Lowry's *Number the Stars* (1989) was the topic for a book club in the class, so David decided to use passages from the novel for repeated reading.

David administered the Flynt-Cooter Reading Inventory for the Classroom (Flynt & Cooter, 2004) to his 11 students as a pre-test to determine their beginning reading rate, (measured in words per minute), and word accuracy (determined by reading miscues). Then, he explained what they would do each week for the next six weeks to become better readers. On Mondays, each student in the class would read a narrative passage twice and then set a weekly goal for his or her reading rate.

On a typical Monday, David modeled fluent reading of each student's new passage while the student followed along silently. Often, a student would ask him to repeat a word that they did not recognize or were not sure how to pronounce. The student then read the passage while David recorded reading rate and miscues. Afterwards, he reviewed miscues with the student. Then, David had the student read the passage a second time to reinforce difficult words. With this introduction to the passage in mind, the student set his or her weekly reading-rate goal. David helped students modify their goals when necessary. This entire process typically took four to six minutes for each student.

On Tuesday, Wednesday, and Thursday, the student read the passage one time aloud to David, after which he reviewed miscues with the student. This took only two or three minutes per student. On Friday, David recorded reading rate and miscues while the student read the passage. Then David and the student reviewed the reading progress recorded on the graph to determine whether the weekly goal was met.

"It was a very big deal," David says. "The motivation factor of reaching a goal was tremendous." The good news was, even when a student didn't reach his or her goal, all students had some success, because they could see their improvement on the graph.

Working individually with 11 students took most of David's time. Fortunately, he had a paraprofessional whom he trained to conduct the repeated readings on Tuesday, Wednesday, and Thursday so he could instruct students on other important skills such as comprehension and writing.

At the end of the six-week study, David administered the post-test (Flynt & Cooter, 2004), and was not surprised to find that the students showed statistically significant improvement in rate and accuracy. In January 2006, David's research was published in *Reading Horizons* (Paige, 2006). The abstract on the ERIC website (eric.ed.gov) states the implications for teachers as follows:

> The study results suggest that for the classroom teacher, daily, extended use of a repeated reading intervention with above-grade-level passages may have two positive effects on students with reading disabilities. First, reading rate may increase, meaning that a greater volume of text can be read, enabling a student to read more productively. Secondly, a decrease in reading miscues may also occur, resulting in greater decoding accuracy and aiding comprehension. These two factors may improve overall reading efficiency.

Action Research Study: Choral Reading

Although he had seen choral reading cited frequently as a method to improve fluency, David found there were very few actual studies. So for his next study, he decided to measure the effects of choral reading with a new class of learning-disabled sixth-grade readers. Again, David used the Flynt-Cooter (2004) as a pre-test measure for reading rate and word accuracy in this group of 16 students. David picked passages from three African folktales to use over the six-week period, one for each week. On Mondays, David modeled fluent reading of the passage for the class, after which they read the passage as "one voice" while the tape recorder ran. After this brief fluency practice, David continued with his normal instructional routine, which included a mix of small group activities like guided reading, explicit skill instructions, and writing. For the rest of the week, the class practiced the choral reading passage once or twice a day and on Friday made another tape recording.

The goal on Monday was to read with one voice by Friday. The tape recording proved to be an extremely valuable tool, as the students really responded to hearing their improvement from Monday to Friday.

"Goal setting was highly motivating," David believes. It didn't start out that way, however.

> There was a group of three, sometimes four, boys who just didn't want to take part. By the end of the third week, the reading really started to come together. One day, after a reading, Kayla said, "Mr. Paige, that was *good!*" She was so excited. I thought, "Yeah!" Then the tide started to turn. The boys couldn't stand excluding themselves any longer. They were some of the lowest readers. It suddenly became a big deal for them to participate.

By the end of his experiment, David knew other teachers could easily implement repeated, choral reading and thus help their students become better readers. So he submitted the study to an educational journal.

Action Research Study: Reading Rate and Dyslexia

In his master's degree program, David studied the work of Dr. Zvia Breznitz, a neurocognitive researcher. Breznitz's focus on the diagnosis and remediation of learning disabilities was important for David's work with special education students. He was especially interested in her work with dyslexic readers. Breznitz and her colleagues theorize that reading rate affects the quality of comprehension and decoding. "We found that when we pushed a dyslexic child to work faster, within their own limit of capacity of course, we saw that the activation of the brain became much closer to that of regular readers" (Breznitz, 2007). That sounded like fluency research to David!

Once again, repeated readings were used with individual sixth-grade students, but for this study, David pressed one half of the class to read at a faster rate. The other half of the class simply continued with repeated readings. The procedure followed that of the first study, with teacher modeling and student practice on Mondays, then goal setting and daily repeated reading, ending with review of progress on Fridays. The protocol for one student in the experimental group might look like this:

Monday	60 words per minute
Tuesday	Rate to be increased by 5%
Wednesday	Rate to be increased by 5%
Thursday	Rate to be increased by 5%
Friday	Rate should be at 120% of Monday's rate

For the first six weeks, David studied the effect of the acceleration on sight words and decoding. He found no difference in the two groups. Both the students who were pushed to read at an accelerated rate and the students who were doing simple repeated reading showed significant gains in sight-word reading and decoding.

"I was surprised by the results," David notes. "I really expected the acceleration kids to do better than the traditional group. I guess we will drop the idea of an acceleration phenomenon but continue to focus on traditional repeated reading for fluency and comprehension."

Although David's class size had increased in his second study, "Fortunately, I had also gotten more efficient at administering repeated reading." The repeated reading took about the same amount of time per student as in his first study, but David and his paraprofessional rotated through two guided reading groups per day so that in addition to repeated reading, every student had guided reading about three times per week. That year, the school also went to a block schedule, so David's time with each class increased from 55 minutes to 70 minutes. He now had time for mini-lessons on specific skills or for grand conversations about books. David reflects on the research studies:

> In some ways, implementing individual repeated reading strategies was always a balancing act between instruction and classroom management. On the other hand, choral reading was much easier to conduct, and despite the prevalent thinking that all text encounters must be "custom fit" to the student, my data suggested that it still made a positive difference with students. The other element to choral reading is that it is a monitored strategy, meaning the teacher is providing support for all students by leading the class in reading. If a student does not know how to decode a word, they can hear the teacher read it. While this may not be as optimal as one-on-one reading, it still provides considerable support for the reader, particularly when combined with subsequent guided reading instruction. My instructional fight-song is "time on text!"

The Next Study

David would like to know if and how repeated reading can improve comprehension through oral retellings. Using a model from Trabasso and Suh (1993) to assess the comprehension of oral retellings, he wonders:

> What's making them improve? Besides just knowing that the retelling improved, I'd like to identify exactly where it got better. I want to know if the student was better at describing the setting, or the outcome, or something else. At the end of the year I will have a longitudinal study where I can compare the total scores to see what else I can learn.

Evidence of Success

David believes all teachers should include a fluency component in their reading instruction. He advises:

> Choral reading is easy to implement. It doesn't take a lot of instructional time and kids like it a lot. I'd recommend the Monday to Friday approach and use the tape recording strategy. Get kids involved with tracking their progress. That really works.

David is "absolutely passionate" about teacher research and believes all teachers should be involved in a project in their own classrooms each year. He explains his position this way:

> How many faculty meetings do we sit in and hear someone say "research-based"? Often it isn't backed up, and we don't know it, so anything flies. It's become a very loose term. If more teachers did action research maybe we'd have more substance. There's so much benefit. David rattles off a list: First, you really get to know your kids. Second, you get to investigate something of interest to you. Third, you get a high feeling of professionalism. It's invigorating! Fourth, it keeps you sharp and informs your teaching. Fifth, you can compare your action research to scientific research.

David concludes his advice for teachers with the following: "I think being both a teacher and a learner can't help but have a positive effect. Research continually makes exciting discoveries and insights into how we can help children learn. I think being a reflective teacher goes hand-in-glove with being a learner; one can't happen without the other."

Reflections

1. David Paige states, "Half of my students should not be in this class. They got behind early on and have never caught up." What kinds of changes to student assessment can prevent misplacement of struggling readers without learning disabilities into special educations?

2. Are there students whose reading difficulties puzzle you? Describe them. What could you do to gain more insight into their difficulties?

3. How often do students do repeated reading in your classroom? How do you make the decision as to when they do it?

4. David Paige states, "When we stretch ourselves as learners, we ignite and recharge." What do you do to stretch yourself as a learner?

5. When was the last time you heard someone use the term *research-based*? How do you feel when you hear that term?

You're a
Grand Old Flag
Fluency and Social Studies
in Mesquite, Texas

Assisted reading involves the student reading a text while simultaneously hearing it read to him or her by a more fluent reader. The integration of seeing a text while simultaneously hearing it can have a profound impact on the student's ability to recognize the words in text accurately and fluently (Rasinski & Hoffman, 2003).

A common and effective form of assisted reading is choral reading. Choral reading, whether as whole-group, antiphonal (parts are read by different groups), or echo reading, allows the more fluent readers in a group to provide support for their less fluent classmates. It is a wonderful way to build group spirit and cohesion. Many texts, such as poems, song lyrics, school and class cheers, and quotations lend themselves to choral reading. The key to choral reading, as with any form of fluency activity, is to insure that the students have access to the written text and are prompted to actually read it, even if they already have it memorized (Fawcett & Rasinski, 2008).

Patriotic Songs and Poems as Fluency Practice

With No Child Left Behind breathing down their necks, reading and math teachers might envy their social studies counterparts just a little, since NCLB does not include social studies as one of the high-stakes tests for determining which schools fail to make the grade. Social studies teachers like DeeAnna Sellards don't miss the testing, but they also regret that social studies consequently "becomes the step child of the subjects" far too often. So when DeeAnna learned a new strategy that would put social studies in the limelight, she was ready to go!

DeeAnna teaches fifth grade in Mesquite, Texas, and state standards require United States history for her students. Recently, she attended a conference where she heard about an instructional strategy that she knew would be perfect for teaching history concepts, improving her students' reading fluency, and showcasing social studies. The strategy simply calls for repeated reading of traditional patriotic songs that have somehow become lost on today's schoolchildren.

The Lesson Plan

DeeAnna teaches the lesson as follows:

* Each student receives a copy of song lyrics that support the social studies concept being studied.

* DeeAnna reads the lyrics as students follow along. She talks about how song lyrics are like poetry, and she points out her phrasing, expression, and intonation. She stresses to students that "the point of this is to make you better readers."

* The students participate in the reading. Sometimes they echo-read with DeeAnna; sometimes she and they take turns reading every other line; sometimes girls read odd-numbered lines and boys read even-numbered lines; sometimes they choral-read.

* The class discusses the meaning of the song as a whole and how it connects to what they will be studying in history.

* They discuss particular words, phrases, or lines, and they highlight words that are new to them.

* Then, they read the piece as a whole again.

The students practice the lyrics at least twice a day. DeeAnna says, laughing, "They beg, 'Can we do it again?'" The music teacher includes the song in music class. After a day or two, students usually know the song by heart. Then they perform for various audiences.

Choosing the Songs

DeeAnna didn't have trouble finding song lyrics to fit the Texas standards. She found one book with many of the songs she would need, and the music teacher was delighted to assist. Lyrics to "The Star-Spangled Banner" were in the social studies textbook.

When students studied U.S. symbols, DeeAnna kicked off the unit with "You're a Grand Old Flag." "The Star-Spangled Banner" accompanied a unit on the founding of America. DeeAnna found a song that supported the study of colonial America that actually contained the names of all 13 colonies. When studying the Revolutionary War, students learned the lyrics of "America the Beautiful" and "Auld Lang Syne," hailing back to the lines from "You're a Grand Old Flag": "Should auld acquaintance be forgot, Keep your eye on that grand old flag." For Constitution Day, the students learned the Preamble to the U.S. Constitution and performed it not as a song but as Readers Theater (see pages 80–81).

Performance

DeeAnna's principal, Becky Rasco, is really excited about what the fifth graders are learning. She had gone to a similar staff development presentation the previous year and saw the potential for such a strategy, so she was happy to help DeeAnna get some needed materials. She invited the students to perform regularly on the school's live video announcements.

Students have also performed for other classes and at PTA meetings. When they performed "You're a Grand Old Flag" for their parents, the response was overwhelmingly positive. DeeAnna explains, "Our school is in a low-income area and we don't always get a lot of parent response. Not only did many parents show up for the performance, but they were excited to hear their students sing songs they had learned as kids."

History Lessons That Accompany the Songs

Patriotic songs in and of themselves are enough to increase reading fluency, but be assured DeeAnna plans effective history lessons that tie it all together. She explains:

> I'm big on making connections. They remember it when things are connected. If we are reading a story, I try to make connections to something in current events. For example, we made connections between the Boston Tea Party and the Montgomery Bus Boycott. We connected our study of the Revolutionary War to Iraq. They've become so used to connections that I don't even have to do it. *They* make the connections. It's the same with the songs. It's not just me teaching social studies. What I'm doing supports reading.

DeeAnna's history lessons incorporate skills they are learning in language arts, such as cause and effect, compare and contrast, and text-to-text connections. In addition, she and the language arts teacher work together for the required language arts research project.

Evidence of Success

Fluent reading has extended beyond the patriotic songs in DeeAnna's school. Every teacher on the fifth-grade team has commented that students are reading more in phrases rather than word by word. The fifth-grade reading teacher is especially pleased with how the students' reading has improved.

DeeAnna also believes the project has helped to develop students' vocabulary. "They have gotten familiar with bigger words. Think of the national anthem, 'The Star-Spangled Banner.' There are a lot of vocabulary words there."

Self-esteem has improved for some students, and DeeAnna attributes that to the songs project. Priscilla was retained twice before entering fifth grade. Prior to this, she "sat in a corner and did not participate in anything." After she was chosen to perform during the school announcements, a transformation took place. Priscilla, a student who had previously refused to do her work, started contributing in class and brought her grades up to passing. Her former teachers were "amazed that she would even get on the announcements."

DeeAnna attributes all this success to the fact that the students love the strategy. "We have a large Hispanic population, and many of them are very musically inclined. A group of boys acted, on their own, to put 'You're a Grand Old Flag' to a rap beat and then performed it. I haven't had anyone who doesn't want to do it," DeeAnna claims. "Some will moan and groan at first, and then they put it to rap!"

Other teachers in the building have now started using poems, songs, and Readers Theater with their students as well, and performances on morning announcements are becoming more varied. Recently, DeeAnna talked to a first-year teacher about the possibilities. "If you give them purpose, they'll work hard for you. We're not just teaching for a test. It's giving us a purpose."

Future Goals

One goal DeeAnna has established for herself is consistency. She echoes what many teachers feel about an overloaded school day. "Sometimes I have to push it aside because so many other things are going on. I need more time in the day to get it all done. I wouldn't even care if they paid me. I just need more time."

DeeAnna also wants results documented. She is looking forward to the mid-year assessment the reading teacher gives. She is confident it will show measurable results.

At the end of the year, each student will be presented with an "American Songbook" with all the lyrics they have learned throughout the year. There's little doubt that years from now, when students look back on their songbooks, they will not only be able to sing "You're a Grand Old Flag," but they'll remember the history lesson that went along with it. DeeAnna sums it up: "Our kids have done some fantastic things. We're really proud of them. It's been an inspiration for me."

Reflections

1. Is fluency relegated to the language arts block in your classroom? Describe a content area lesson that incorporates fluency instruction.

2. Make a list of all the patriotic songs and poems you have heard over the years.

3. Look at the state standards for your grade level. Can you match the songs and poems you listed in #2 with major social studies concepts?

4. What examples of choral reading do you observe in your school at different grade levels?

5. DeeAnna Sellards would like documentation that her patriotic songs and poems project is impacting reading achievement. What steps would you suggest she take to gather such evidence?

Readers Theater:
The Preamble to the U.S. Constitution

A Choral Reading in Seven Voices

BY LORRAINE GRIFFITH

R1: The Constitution of the United States of America.

All: We the people . . .

R2: The people: First the Native American,

R3: then a flood of Europeans immigrants, Africans,

R4: Middle Easterners,

R5: Asian peoples,

R6: South Americans,

R7: and they keep on coming.

All: We the people of the United States . . .

R1: The United States: ALL 50!

R2: From Portland, Maine, west to San Diego, California,

R3: from Fargo, North Dakota, south to El Paso, Texas,

R4: Alaska, and Hawaii.

All: We the people of the United States, in order to form a more perfect Union . . .

R5: That Union seemed perfect, all of the colonies became states, as well as the territories to the west,

R6: until the southern states seceded because they wanted states' rights.

R7: But the Civil War ended with a more perfect union of states based upon the belief that all Americans deserved the right to life, liberty, and the pursuit of happiness.

All: We the people of the United States, in order to form a more perfect Union, establish justice . . .

R1: Justice was ensured for Americans by establishing a court system beginning with local courthouses and moving up to the Supreme Court in Washington, D.C.

All: We the people of the United States, in order to form a more perfect Union, establish justice, ensure domestic tranquility . . .

R2: There have been times when our nation's tranquility has been disturbed.

R3: But in spite of Pearl Harbor, December 7th, 1941,

R4: and as recent as the horror of September 11th,

R5: we still live in a stable and peaceful country.

All: We the people of the United States, in order to form a more perfect Union, establish justice, ensure domestic tranquility, provide for the common defense . . .

R6: The Air Force. No one comes close! Soar to new heights in the wild blue yonder!

R7: The Army. Be all you can be! Be an army of one! Hoo-ah!

R1: The Navy. Welcome aboard. Anchors aweigh!

R2: The Coast Guard. Protecting America. It's our job every day!

Readers Theater: The Preamble to the U.S. Constitution *(Continued)*

R3: And the Marines. The few, the proud. Semper Fi *(Figh)*!

All: **We the people of the United States, in order to form a more perfect Union, establish justice, ensure domestic tranquility, provide for the common defense, promote the general welfare . . .**

R4: People's basic needs must be met in a country.

R5: Needs for housing, education, transportation, and health care are overseen by our government system.

R6: Labor laws ensure that people work in safe environments and that they are paid fairly for the work that they do.

All: **We the people of the United States, in order to form a more perfect Union, establish justice, ensure domestic tranquility, provide for the common defense, promote the general welfare, and secure the blessings of liberty to ourselves . . .**

R1: Jefferson's promise of Life, Liberty, and the Pursuit of Happiness came later for many of the peoples of our nation.

R2: African Americans did not share the rights of whites by law until the Emancipation Proclamation was signed in 1863.

R3: Women did not share in the rights of men to vote or own property until 1920 when the Suffrage Act was ratified.

All: **We the people of the United States, in order to form a more perfect Union, establish justice, ensure domestic tranquility, provide for the common defense, promote the general welfare, and secure the blessings of liberty to ourselves and our posterity . . .**

R1: That's you and me!

R2-3: And our children!

R4-7: And our children's children!

R1-7: And their children, too!

All: **We the people of the United States, in order to form a more perfect Union, establish justice, ensure domestic tranquility, provide for the common defense, promote the general welfare, and secure the blessings of liberty to ourselves and our posterity, do ordain and establish this Constitution for the United States of America.**

R5: The Constitution of the United States of America has stood the test of time.

R6: Although it was signed on September 17th, 1787, it still stands as a ruling document of laws, ensuring our rights and liberties that we still enjoy today.

R7: And so, let us proclaim once again for all the world to hear…

R1: The Preamble to the Constitution of the United States of America.

R2-3: We the people of the United States, in order to form a more perfect Union,

R4-6: establish justice, ensure domestic tranquility, provide for the common defense, promote the general welfare,

All: **and secure the blessings of liberty, to ourselves and our posterity, do ordain and establish this Constitution for the United States of America.**

Adapted from Rasinski, T. V., & Griffith, L. (2005). Texts for Fluency Practice.

Reading
Morality Stories
to Convey Meaning
in Kissimmee, Florida

Prosody is a word we don't often encounter. Using appropriate prosody is synonymous with reading with expression, which, in turn, "refers to the way oral reading sounds and silent reading feels. It has to do with the 'music' that accompanies fluent reading" (Walker, Mokhtari & Sargent, 2006, p. 90).

An examination of professional literature shows that "definitions of oral reading fluency must include three components—accuracy, automaticity, and prosody" (Mathson, Allington & Solic, 2006, p. 116; see also Kuhn & Stahl, 2004, p. 416). Together, they can be used to "build a bridge to comprehension" (Rasinski, 2004b, p. 46). Assessment instruments such as DIBELS (Good & Kaminski, 2005) draw attention to the first two components, but the third is more difficult to quantify, and therefore is more likely to be overlooked in an age of heightened accountability. Our efforts to help struggling readers speed through brief passages, word lists, and non-word phonemic exercises may have an effect that we never intended: "A decontextualized instructional focus on exact word recognition may lead students further from literacy, because their motivation becomes correct word calling rather than making sense of what they read" (Mathson, Allington & Solic, 2006, p. 110). The title of an article in *Reading Research Quarterly* by S. Jay Samuels asks a very important question: "The DIBELS Tests: Is Speed of Barking at Print What We Mean by Reading Fluency?" (2007).

To help teachers identify the specific aspects of prosody, Jerry Zutell and Timothy Rasinski (1991, p. 215) introduced the Multidimensional Fluency Scale (MFS). The format for the scale was further developed for classroom use by Kimberly Monfort, a third-grade teacher (2005d, p. 11). See the reproducible on page 23.

Teachers can use the MFS to assess children's oral reading across four dimensions:

*   Expression and volume
*   Phrasing

*   Smoothness
*   Pace

Based on the students' scores on the rubric, teachers are able to tailor instructional activities to meet the developmental needs of individual students. As Rasinski and Padak point out, the MFS "is also useful for helping students evaluate their own reading and in developing their own understanding of fluency in reading" (2005d, p. 11).

What's so important about prosody? Well, it can indicate that the reader is devoting attention to interpreting the material. Hearing someone present an oral rendition of text in a meaningful way gives evidence that the reader is making a connection between words and meaning. With the three components of fluent oral reading in mind, let's consider the possible results of an over-emphasis on accuracy and automaticity, together with a de-emphasis on prosody: We can only wonder, for example, what the Gettysburg Address would have sounded like if Abraham Lincoln had focused on reading rate instead of meaning. Or, what if we asked Katherine Paterson to read a passage from *Bridge to Terabithia* (1977) as quickly as she can without any errors so that we may determine her reading ability?

Prosody must not be overlooked. Melanie Kuhn and Steven Stahl have summed it up nicely in their extensive review of research: Prosodic features "provide clues to an otherwise invisible process; they act as indicators of the reader's comprehension. Given that a fluent reader is one that groups text into syntactically appropriate phrases, this parsing of text signifies that the reader has an understanding of what is being read" (2004, p. 418).

Are there ways to shift the emphasis from measuring a reader's accuracy and automaticity and concentrate instead on making connections between prosody and understanding? What might this focus on prosody look like in a classroom?

Comprehension, Fluency, and the Morality Story

Diana Triplett works with students in grades 6 to 8 at Neptune Middle School in Kissimmee, Florida. About half of the 1,500 students speak Spanish as their first language, and of those, 15 to 20 percent are recent immigrants from Puerto Rico or South America. Diana, who has taught for many years at various grade levels, is currently a literacy coach, primarily responsible for assisting the 30 people who are teaching reading at the school. As a member of the School Wide Assessment Team (called "SWAT" for short), she oversees Neptune's state-mandated oral reading assessments.

For several years, Diana has facilitated activities in which students create scripts from morality stories. Within small groups, learners explore the author's writing style and their own connections to the text, practice reading aloud with expression, and then seek to communicate meaning and prompt discussion through oral reading to their classmates.

The Lesson Plan

"Kids know what kids sound like. That's why I like to find short stories that have dialogues between children," says Diana. "My favorite text for this purpose is Patricia Polacco's *My*

Rotten Redheaded Older Brother (1994). It contains lots of dialogue, and is fairly easy reading for sixth graders. I think it is important to start with an easy text so the students focus on expression and meaning."

Cues for Phrasing

"I begin by modeling reading with expression, and then we do a choral reading of the picture book passages on the overhead," explains Diana. "During these lessons, we focus on cues the author provides for phrasing and expression. This is primarily punctuation (which most of my lower-level students ignore), but also includes word choice, she says. "For example, in the Polacco text, at one point, the brother 'jeered' at the sister. At another point, during an argument, he 'whispered,' even though the phrase includes an exclamation mark. The kids can't just jump into the small group work without the whole-class oral reading and guided practice first. I also model scripting."

Diana explains how she teaches students to convert a story into a script for multiple voices: "I make an overhead transparency of the story and project it on the screen for the class to see. Using colored markers on the first part of the story, we decide where the parts could be divided for two different readers. Then, half the class reads one part and half the other, she says. "Nowadays, if there is a document camera in the room, I can use it to put the script on a whiteboard. I can then mark on my copy of the script or I can use dry-erase markers directly on the board. If there is a projector hooked up to a computer, I can use a word processing program to put the text into different colors for the class." Diana also indicates that a SMART Board can be used if one is available. That way, the teacher can go directly onto the Internet to find a story.

Focus on Meaning

"We concentrate on *meaning* as the class and I examine the text, says Diana. "We talk about logical ways to plan an oral presentation of a story so that the listeners can make sense out of it. As I said before, we look at cues the author used, like punctuation, sentence structure, and paragraph formatting. I have found that the students start to think deeply about the author's craft. How does the author get the point across? Whose voice is telling the story? Who does the reader see or hear?

"This, by the way, is where prosody comes in. What does the text sound like? How can the phrases be read out loud so that people can understand what is going on? These are the questions that the students ask themselves about the stories they encounter.

"Once they are comfortable with the idea of marking a text to make it into a script and are aware of the need to read with prosody, we move on to grade-level text—often an excerpt from an adolescent novel. Jerry Spinelli is a favorite author for this work. I find a variety of different stories so that small groups can present new things to the class. I give copies of the text to a group of four or five students. They take responsibility for splitting up the material and deciding who will read each part. Depending on the number of characters in a story, some people take the roles of multiple narrators, or they read the descriptions of settings or the internal thoughts of a character; other times, there will be choral reading with voices coming in at particular times determined by the group.

"The entire activity takes three or four time periods of 45 minutes each—one period for the teacher to model and guide in a whole group setting, one or two periods to script and rehearse in small groups, and one period to perform and discuss with the class. The members of each small group revisit their text in an authentic way as they prepare their presentations. They practice in order to help each other work on their parts, and then present the stories with an aim toward communicating important ideas."

Finding Text That Is Meaningful to Students

"It's very important to find text that lends itself to this kind of activity," says Diana. "I like using morality stories. These can be very meaningful for students. They are often about situations that people encounter in their lives, situations in which they have to make decisions or reflect on their actions. These engaging stories prompt students to find the main idea and to explore the author's purpose. 'What's the moral of this story?' students ask each other.

"Let me give you an example. Several times, I've used a story about a very intelligent dog. In brief: A dog walks into a butcher shop with a paper bag full of money. The butcher takes the money and puts meat in the bag. The dog returns home, somehow knowing which bus to take. When he gets home, he knocks on the window so that his owner will open the door. The dog's owner beats the dog—furious that the dog forgot to take his house key when he went to the butcher shop. When I've asked my sixth graders, 'What's the moral of this story?,'" says Diana, "they invariably say, 'People shouldn't be cruel to animals.' Can't they go deeper than that? We need to give them opportunities to go beyond literal and surface-level meanings. Children I've encountered in the past 20 years seem to have had very little experience examining the meaning of stories."

A Few Sources for Morality Stories

Picture Books

Burleigh, R. (2006). *Tiger of the snows: Tenzing Norgay: The boy whose dream was Everest.*

Hoffman, M. (1991). *Amazing Grace.*

Mora, P. (1997). *The race of Toad and Deer.*

Muth, J. J. (2002). *The three questions: Based on a story by Leo Tolstoy.*

Polacco, P. (1994). *My rotten redheaded older brother.*

Novels

Bloor, E. (1997). *Tangerine.*

Cooney, C. B. (1987). *Among friends.*

Creech, S. (1994). *Walk two moons.*

Gorman, C. (1999). *Dork in disguise.*

Paterson, K. (1977). *Bridge to Terabithia.*

Spinelli, J. (2003). *Milkweed.*

Woodson, J. (2000). *Miracle's boys.*

Morality stories can be found in many places. Aesop's fables or multicultural folktales would work, as well as more modern works, like some of those we've named above. Eventually, students could write their own morality tales. Teachers can carefully select brief stories from the Internet and then help students create scripts in an electronic format. Picture books and collections of short stories are available at the library. This script-making activity can also be done with the first few pages of young adult novels such as *Dork in Disguise* (Gorman, 1999) and other coming-of-age stories, as a way to prompt students to read the complete book in the future.

Dual-language books and materials, such as *Tomás and the Library Lady* (Mora, 1997), in which code-switching between languages is used in dialogue, can honor the native-language expertise of English language learners. Oral presentations can provide perfect opportunities to help ELL students develop an awareness of the intonational patterns that are different among languages (Lems, 2006, p. 236). Students can even write original stories in their first language that their classmates then translate into English, as they did in schools in the Toronto metropolitan area, where vast numbers of languages are represented (Chow & Cummins, 2003). This could also be a wonderful source for material to be read aloud.

A Purpose for Reading With Prosody

Diana suggests that teachers look into "critical literacy" (see *Democracy and Education*; Henkin, Dipinto & Hunt, 2002). Diana especially recommends the book *Deeper Reading* (2004) by Kelly Gallagher, a high school teacher from Anaheim, California. In it, Gallagher shares how children can get great satisfaction from exploring the implicit intentions and assumptions of a text and from connecting their own lives to what they read. This motivates students to read with prosody—their purpose is to convey meaning and to engage their peers in an exploration of the morals behind the stories.

In the past, Diana taught a course called "Middle School 101" that every student in the sixth grade was required to take. The class focused on study skills, social skills, character education, and reading. As one can imagine, morality stories played a big part in the curriculum. "I wish we had more time to do innovative activities like these," Diana laments, "but we are obliged to focus a great deal of our energies on testing and gathering data."

Evidence of Success

"I've used fluency rubrics and performance rubrics to give feedback to students, and have seen great improvement over time," notes Diana (see page 88). "Due to the fact that I trained in performance poetry with *Poetry Alive!* (2007), I teach the kids the basic performance stance and include that in the rubric as well. By the way, performance poetry is another great way to practice oral reading fluency.

"As a literacy coach, I have been working with alternative certification teachers who often know little about fluency. I used the picture-book choral reading activity with seventh and eighth graders to introduce fluency to the teachers and their students. The students had been generally bored with the oral reading assessments that we do, but they were very enthusiastic about this kind of oral reading."

"It is difficult for me to come up with evidence of success because I only work with these students briefly as I model for their teachers," Diana continues. "However, over the course of the three or four class periods I work with them, I see increased motivation and engagement. Of course, I don't usually see an increase in their reading rate, but I do hear improvement in prosody, and students report that they understand the text better. I think this is because they willingly spend time rereading and thinking deeply about meaning. Voluntarily rereading text is not something that I normally see in striving readers. In fact, they are most likely to skim a passage superficially and believe that they are finished whether or not they understood the text. When they create their own scripts for Readers Theater or performance poetry, they *want* to reread, and they are very focused on meaning. Their performances are polished. Even the English language learners read expressively."

As students realize that the purpose of reading aloud is to convey meaning, not simply to "read quickly" or to "score better on a test," Diana has found that they are more engaged in the exploration of written material. Reading for real purposes has helped these youngsters focus on ways that authors write. It has helped to motivate them to write their own stories and to become more literate individuals—obviously a major goal we have as teachers. What's more, it can help to reinvigorate our teaching as we accompany children on their voyages of discovery.

Reflections

1. How can teachers place an emphasis on the connection between comprehension and fluency?

2. How can this book about fluency (or the materials from the reference list) be used for teacher-designed professional development activities?

3. What would it require for you or your students to make a script out of an already existing story or other text? What benefits would result from writing scripts?

4. Plan a week's instructional sequence in scripting and performing. What materials would you use? What would you do each day of the week?

Readers Theater Presentation Rubric

Student Name: _____ Date: _____

CATEGORY	4	3	2	1
Participation	Student participates enthusiastically, cooperating with group members and providing assistance to others in the group.	Student participates in group presentation, but does not help group to prepare presentation.	Student participates some, but sits down before the performance is complete.	Student does not participate.
Fluency	Student reads part smoothly with good expression.	Student reads part, at times varying voice for expression.	Student reads part with few errors but uses little expression.	Student reads in a monotone voice.
Performance	Student uses a performance stance and stays in character for the entire presentation.	Student uses a performance stance most of the time, but sometimes steps out of character to talk with other group members or classmates.	Student does not use performance stance consistently. Student may wander or engage in conversation with others during the performance.	Student slouches during performance and does not show an awareness of audience. Student may talk or argue with classmates during presentation.
Voice	Student speaks loudly and clearly. Student can be easily heard and understood from any part of the room.	Student speaks loudly and clearly most of the time.	Student's voice is low and difficult to hear most of the time.	Student cannot be heard or understood.

Total Score: _____ /16

Source: Rubric developed by Diana Triplett, Neptune Middle School, Kissimmee, Florida, from a RubiStar format (rubistar.4teachers.org).

Using
Harry Potter for
Sixth-Grade Readers Theater
in Oswego, Illinois

Having students create their own scripts from a story provides them with valuable literacy experience that Timothy V. Rasinski calls "variable scaffolding" (2004a, p. 114). In this way, stronger writers can rearrange a story into a lively script, while developing writers can participate by turning part of a narrative into dialogue form. Everyone can take part in making these scripts at the appropriate level. Readers Theater scripts can be created by students or by teachers and can also be found in books and on the Internet (Shepherd, 2009).

When a script is created, it is time for fluency practice. Readers Theater is one of the best methods of practicing fluency (Carrick, 2006) and is becoming increasingly popular in classrooms around the U.S. and in Australia, New Zealand, and other English-speaking countries. Carrick (2000) found that fifth-grade students engaging in Readers Theater groups had greater gains in fluency and word accuracy than students in a paired reading setting or using a traditional basal.

Heading Off to Hogwarts

Kate Gallinatti is a new teaching assistant in a sixth-grade classroom at Karl Plank Junior High in Oswego, Illinois. She only heard of fluency instruction for the first time last fall, in a university class about teaching reading with English language learners. However, Kate boldly decided to take the plunge and taught a one-week-long fluency-centered unit to her sixth-grade students. Based on a key narrative passage in the final Harry Potter book, *Harry Potter and the Deathly Hallows* (Rowling, 2007), Kate created a well-designed Readers Theater project through which she also showcased her teaching skills, not only for the teacher in whose classroom she assists, but for her students, her assistant principal, and a visiting video camera crew!

A **Close-Up** Look Into **15 Diverse Classrooms**

89

A few hundred pages into the nearly 1,000-page book lies a story, "The Tale of the Three Brothers," that is supposed to have been taken from a book of stories, much loved by wizards, called *The Tales of Beedle the Bard* (later published as a standalone book). In the story reminiscent of "The Three Billy Goats Gruff," the brothers' lives are in danger as they try to cross a bridge. The story provides important clues that ultimately guide the reader toward cracking the mystery of the *Deathly Hallows'* thrilling denouement. Kate undertook the project partly because she enjoyed the Harry Potter books so much and partly because she discovered that none of her students had read them yet! She hoped the project might pique their interest. She also recognized the benefits of Readers Theater for upper elementary students (Martinez, Roser & Strecker, 1999), not only for the social dimension that repeated reading provides, but also for the motivation it generates in students whose interest in outside reading is beginning to decline as they move out of elementary school.

The Lesson Plan

Kate's weeklong instructional sequence, aligned with the state language arts standards, consisted of an hour each day for five days. Before the first day, she broke the story into four pieces because she knew it would be too long for the students to turn into a script. She also prepared a rubric (see page 94) that they would use to analyze their own performances as well as the whole unit. And she obtained multiple copies of a wordless picture book from the library that could be used to model script writing.

> **DAY 1:** Kate engaged students in a conversation about what elements make up a play or script. She provided copies of the wordless picture book *Frog, Where Are You?* by Mercer Mayer (1969) to pairs of students. She led them through a few pages of the book as a whole class, asking students to create lines of dialogue based on what the pictures looked like, and writing the lines on a flipchart. After the modeling, the students continued creating their own scripts of the wordless story.

> **DAY 2:** Kate handed out typed copies of "The Tale of the Three Brothers" to the students and pre-taught some words related to prosody and dramatic reading. Then she read it for them twice, first expressively, then in a drab, monotonous voice, to highlight "best and worst" practices in oral reading. Students were asked to discuss the differences in her two performances, using the vocabulary about drama and prosody that they had just practiced.

> * Next, she asked volunteers to read their original scripts of *Frog Where Are You?*, and, as a class, to discuss what elements contributed to making the dialogue effective and compelling.

> * With the two elements of expressive reading and creating scripts now well introduced, the students were ready to move on to a greater challenge: turning a narrative passage they had read into a script.

Kate took the first part of "The Tale of the Three Brothers" and modeled how to create dialogue from it for the whole class. Using a think-aloud, she pondered how to capture the gist of part of the story, turn it into lines of dialogue and actions, and faithfully preserve the tone of the passage.

✳ After modeling the process of writing the script, she broke students into four heterogeneous small groups, and each group transformed one part of the story into a script. These groups were to stay together until the performance, and perform the script they themselves had written. The only rule was that each person in the group had to have a speaking role. Kate suggested that they also might want to have a director, narrator, or stage director. "They were only asked which characters were in the first two paragraphs [we had done together] because I wanted each group to set up their script in the way they decided," she explains.

✳ By the end of the day, they had written their scripts and chosen their parts. The scripts were full of lively language, for example, "Middle Brother: Time to go and try out our gifts!" That night, Kate took home the original scripts they had created and typed them all up, double-spaced, in large black font. At school the following morning, she made enough photocopies for each group to practice from.

DAY 3: Students practiced their new scripts, working out stage directions and thinking up props and costumes. They also received the rubric Kate had prepared and talked about what they were going to strive for in their performances. Later on this same day, students created a large, painted background of the bridge, to serve as the set.

DAY 4: There was a lot of rehearsing and repeated reading—the "heavy lifting" of fluency instruction. Students assumed the parts they had written for themselves, practicing their own scripts and polishing their timing, phrasing, and expression. That night, Kate checked out the recording equipment from the school for use the following day. Students, palpably excited, were reminded to bring their costumes and props, along with their families.

DAY 5: At last, it was show time! The costumed students had family in the audience, and school personnel arrived to watch the show as well. The large, painted setting was erected and stabilized and the stage area cleared off. After hurried last rehearsals in the hall, the show got underway. The Readers Theater pieces were performed and videotaped, and bows were taken to enthusiastic applause.

The following day, the students reviewed the video recordings together and critiqued their own performances, using the rubric and feedback forms Kate had created.

Evidence of Success

Kate received overwhelmingly positive feedback about the project from the students'. Here are a few interesting responses to Kate's questions:

How comfortable/familiar were you with the story of "The Tale of the Three Brothers"?

"I did not no anything about the story because I do not read Harry Potter but I think I will start reading it because it sounds very inspiring with lots of action."

What did you like about your group's performance?

"I loved my group's performance. We didn't mess up at all, our volume was good, everything was awesome."

"That we were all in it. We were clear and loud."

"I liked when the oldest brother and the Evil Wizard dueled."

"I liked that we all did what we were instructed to do and acted to our parts and didn't goof off when doing it!"

How comfortable were you with your part?

"I was very good because I practiced every night. Also I practiced every day."

"I memorized all my lines because I read my lines like 15 times."
"I knew my part like the back of my hand."

"I read it plenty of times and memorized it all."

Thinking about only your performance, how did you do with volume, voice, enthusiasm? Also, how would you describe your overall presentation?

"I think that I did the volume, along with my posture, and voice, great. It was very convincing."

"I think the volume was good, we showed a lot of emotion. I think it was good for our first time on the camera!"

Kate plans to continue the Readers Theater performances and hopes to expose her students to different text genres as well, such as poems, short stories, plays, and previously written Readers Theater pieces.

Here are some tips from Kate for those planning a similar unit: "Next time, I would give the students more time to practice their plays 'on stage,' so to speak, before we began filming. I think that this would have made the play 'flow' better. I noticed that the students could have had a little more direction in regards to how to exit and enter a stage. I would also have the students practice reading their story aloud with only one partner a few times, as opposed to the group of six. This would have made it a little bit more intimate, and each student would have had more of an opportunity to read the play more than once in class. Next time, I would have them do a dry run of the play, give them tips on how to improve enthusiasm, voice volume, inflection, etc. That way they would be able to practice the night before the filming."

"Another modification I would make," she continues, "is that next time, before the lesson is even introduced, I would work with a short play beforehand. This way, we would review concepts of dialogue and scripts before the 'big' lesson. This may give the students a bit more background knowledge, and it could ultimately help strengthen the Harry Potter lesson."

Kate says she would utilize more technology as well. For instance, she says, "Maybe we could have some spooky background music to add some effect." She also realized students could type up their own scripts in the computer lab instead of handwriting them and having her type them.

Kate notes, "Having the students reread the story so many times led them to high self-reflection ratings of their reading. Because they had reread it so much, their reflections were positive. Also, seeing the movie was a great way for the students and me to see if our scripts were a hit!"

Kate Gallinatti is a beginning teacher but her integrated fluency lesson is helping her put an important tool into her teacher toolbox that will serve her in years to come. All she needs now is a classroom of her own in which to try her wings!

Reflections

1. Take a short passage or story with which you are familiar, and, with a partner, adapt it into a script. It could even be a short fairy tale or bedtime story. If possible, practice and then perform it for others, just as these students did. Talk about how you felt and what you learned in the process of doing it.

2. When students read from a script, there is usually a narrator. How would you coach a narrator as opposed to those playing character roles? Would eye contact and body language differ? If so, in what way?

3. Discuss imaginative ways that inexpensive props, costumes, and stage settings can be constructed using available materials.

4. Look at Kate's rubric for the Readers Theater performances (p. 94). What would you change if it were a different kind of performance? A different grade level? If it were for English language learners?

5. Share your own experiences with the Harry Potter books. Can you think of ways you could incorporate other scenes or characters from the Harry Potter books in fluency instruction?

Readers Theater Evaluation—Group Scoring

Piece Performed: _____

Author: _____

Group Members: _____

_____

Script (Rate on scale from 1 to 3 with 3 being the highest)

_____ Creativity

_____ Parallels with the original story

_____ Well-defined characters

_____ Well-defined dialogue

_____ Narration

Performance (Rate on scale from 1 to 3 with 3 being the highest)

_____ Direction

_____ Volume

_____ Participation

_____ Flow/pacing

_____ Body language

_____ Props/set

_____ Familiarity with the text (fluency and accuracy)

Total Score: _____ /36

Comments: _____

_____

Teacher Action Research

in Harrisonville, Missouri

There is no shortage of educational research. Often, there is much to be gained from reading about what someone else has studied and to look for applications to one's own classroom. However, sometimes teachers are the best ones, perhaps the only ones, to answer questions about their own classrooms. Teachers who do "action research" raise questions about what is happening in their classrooms. They observe, collect student work, keep careful records, and analyze what they find in order to improve teaching and learning. Some teachers do action research alone, others work with colleagues to study some aspect of teaching at their school. Some design and carry out action research as a requirement in a master's degree course, others informally and intuitively carry out a plan for finding answers to their questions. Teacher research into students' reading fluency or fluency strategies can prove to be a powerful catalyst for improving reading achievement.

Fluency Instruction Begins

Kelly Wernex wanted to know why. Why did so many of the struggling readers in her after-school tutoring sessions read word by word, like robots? Why didn't they use expression? Why did some students read very slowly, while others read so fast their phrasing didn't even make sense? And, most important, why didn't they comprehend what they read? Kelly explains:

> I wasn't up on the research on fluency. It had never been part of our reading curriculum. So I started doing some research. I read some of Timothy Rasinski's articles and some articles in *The Reading Teacher*. I wanted to know exactly what fluency was. I needed to know how it affected reading, and I wanted to know what teaching strategies I could use to help my students become more fluent. When I learned how greatly fluency affects comprehension, well, I knew what I had to do!

After this revelation, Kelly began explicit fluency instruction right away with her after-school struggling readers as well as with her regular fifth-grade class. She told her students that if they became fluent readers, not only would they sound better when they read, but they would also have a much better understanding of what they were reading. She used the term *intonation* and modeled it for them. She explained the importance of rate and convinced them that reading *too slow* hinders their comprehension, but reading *too fast* doesn't always mean better. She put little marks in their texts to help them *chunk* phrases. She read with expression and without expression and asked the students which they liked better and why. Naturally, there was no disagreement on which they preferred. Morgan, a student in her class, explained quite simply, "It sounds boring without fluency."

The students felt like their teacher was letting them in on a secret, and they were excited to try out these skills that were new to them. Taylor said, "I love fluency. It's making me a better reader. I never knew what intonation meant. I seriously love the way Mrs. Wernex explains it. When Mrs. Wernex tells me, I get it."

In addition to providing the language of fluency for her students, Kelly tried some of the teaching strategies she had read about in her research. Her students practiced fluency by choral reading, using Readers Theater scripts, and repeated readings. They practiced self-evaulation (see page 101).

Kelly was so impressed with the progress her students were making in a short time that she went to her principal, Mr. Erholtz, and said, "We need to teach fluency. Our students can decode, and they can read, but they're failing in comprehension, and it's because we aren't teaching fluency." He pledged his support.

Action Research Plan

Kelly is one of three classroom teachers who also serve as literacy coaches for the school. As literacy coaches, they attend training, try new approaches in their classrooms, pilot new curricula, and provide professional development training for the rest of the staff. They also model and observe in classrooms while providing support and resources to teachers. This was the perfect team to expand on what Kelly had started.

She met with the other literacy coaches and presented the idea of doing an action research study for the purpose of answering the question, "Does fluency instruction have an effect on reading comprehension?" Both Kim Spencer and Valerie Levy, third-grade teachers, were interested in investigating and collecting data to support the study. Kelly invited her fifth-grade colleague, Crissy Gilvin, to join her in the action research project. One class would be the test group, receiving the research "treatment" (district reading curriculum along with direct fluency instruction) and the other class would be the control group, receiving only the regular reading curriculum. They would gather data to see if the fluency instruction made a difference. Thus, the action research consisted of two experimental groups and two control groups, one type of each from grades 3 and 5.

Fluency Treatment

The treatment groups received direct fluency instruction. Kelly states:

> The best part is that we pulled it into our regular instruction. Plan and preparation time was less than 10 minutes a week. We didn't need an extra 45 minutes of reading time. It fit right in with what we were already doing! Teachers shouldn't think, "Fluency is something else I have to plan for and teach."

Every Monday, teachers of the experimental groups provided 10 to 15 minutes of directed fluency instruction using *Fluency Lessons for the Overhead* (Sweeney, 2004a, 2004b). Students were presented with excerpted works of favorite authors Jack Prelutsky, Seymour Simon, Robert Munsch, Jane Yolen, and others. They used those excerpts to practice intonation, rate, phrasing, and automaticity in word recognition. Each excerpt included comprehension activities and independent fluency practice.

Weekly Fluency Practice

Throughout the week, students participated in a variety of fluency activities. The teachers continually reminded students of the connections between fluency and the reading activities. Activities included:

* Books on tape
* Repeated readings
* Choral reading
* Partner reading
* Echo reading

One activity the students especially enjoyed was tape-recording their own reading. After recording, they listened to the tape, self-assessed, reread, and started the cycle again until they were satisfied with their improvement.

Fluency Homework

Each week, students were given homework from *Week-by-Week Homework for Building Reading Comprehension and Fluency* (Rose, 2004). Each student took home a short passage to practice for fluency, with companion comprehension activities to do with a family member.

Weekly Culmination

At the end of every week, students performed a Readers Theater for various audiences. Sometimes they did it for another class, sometimes for their parents, sometimes for the principal, and sometimes just for one another.

Evidence of Success

Before fluency instruction began, the teacher-researchers assessed all four classes using Developmental Reading Assessment (DRA) (Beaver, 1999), the STAR Early Literacy program, and 3-Minute Reading Assessments (Rasinski & Padak, 2005c, 2005d). All assessments were repeated at the end of the year. In addition, students were assessed monthly using 3-Minute Reading Assessments. These assessments provided comparison data to determine if fluency instruction was making a difference.

The data conclusions showed that from a research standpoint, statistically significant differences could not be determined because of the small sample size. Another limitation to the study was the number of students for whom there was incomplete data. However, the fluency groups had average gains or improvements in reading test scores from fall to spring assessments that were greater than the gains in the control groups. With that, the teachers were encouraged because the results pointed in the right direction.

There was a positive relationship between words correct per minute (rate) and comprehension. There was also a positive relationship between rate and scores on STAR, DRA level, DRA accuracy, and DRA comprehension. Fluency expression also correlated with other broader measures of reading performance.

In addition to the quantitative data, the teacher-researchers gathered qualitative data from students, parents, and each other as the project progressed.

Students were asked two specific questions about fluency: (1) What was your favorite fluency activity? (2) Do you think working on fluency helped you become a better reader? Many students expressed a sense of confidence and accomplishment:

> **Reagan:** I liked when we all read together [choral reading] to practice for our reading buddies. Fluency helped me become a better reader because when I used to read to someone, I would stutter—it helped me to get used to reading to someone older and younger than me.
>
> **Taylor:** I think fluency has really helped me become a better reader. It helps me use expression and feeling. It has made me the type of reader I didn't know I could be.
>
> **Clayton:** I learned how to have expression in my reading, and when I read it makes the article or story sound a lot better.
>
> **Brianna:** Fluency has helped me improve my reading by reading at a speed we talk at. I like to look at quotes [dialogue] and change my voice when characters are speaking.

Parents were pleased with the progress their children made.

> **Mrs. H.:** I liked working on it with her. It made both of us more aware when she was reading. The big difference I have seen is when she is now reading aloud, she pays attention to dialogue in the book, changing her voice when there is some.

Ms. F.: I do feel like the fluency instruction is really helping Henry. I just asked him to explain to me what it means to be a fluent reader and he said, "It means reading with expression. If there's an exclamation point, read it with excitement. If there's a question mark, raise your voice at the end. If there's a period, stop, then go on." So, if that's what fluency means to you all, he's got it.

Kim Spencer, the third-grade teacher who joined Kelly in teaching a treatment group reflects:

> I was really impressed with the difference in my students' oral reading. Students who were already reading at or above grade level tended to read fairly monotone at the beginning of the school year. When you would ask them about their reading, they thought they read well, because they didn't have any difficulties decoding words and they usually understood what they read. As we began to talk about the characteristics of a "good" reader, about expression, the importance of paying attention to punctuation, and how punctuation affects understanding, the students started applying these skills to their daily reading. Most of them could see the difference that it made in their oral reading, especially when they were reading to their kindergarten buddies. In turn, they were able to explore fiction text better because they paid attention to how the author intended the text to be written. I feel like I really saw the benefits of fluency instruction with students who tended to be decoding and/or comprehending below grade level.

Future Goals

Kelly, her research partners, and her principal have continued the research and are now in their third year. Direct fluency instruction is now implemented in all classrooms in the building, so data can be collected quarterly for the entire student body. The literacy coaches have given several professional development sessions to help teachers understand fluency and how to teach it in their rooms. Recently they held a "Fluency Night" at the school and invited parents to hear what fluency is, how it affects reading comprehension, what instruction teachers are giving in the classroom, and how parents can help at home. The highlight of the evening was when students modeled Readers Theater for the parents (see page 102).

Kelly and her team's goal is to show statistically significant improvement in their students' reading as a result of fluency instruction. They intend to present it as a reading improvement strategy for the entire district. At the same time, they are implementing a new language arts textbook adoption. Kelly says, "Fluency instruction fits pretty well with the new adoption. The new program includes modeled reading, shared reading, and guided reading. It's what you do with fluency strategies, so what we are doing should work well with the entire district."

Reflections

1. What are the barriers to conducting action research?

2. How can the barriers be overcome?

3. What are some benefits of conducting action research?

4. Think about reading fluency in your classroom. Is there a particular student you want to understand better? Would you like to know if a certain fluency strategy is really working? Do you want to know the effects of parent involvement? What do you wonder about? Write three questions.

5. Choose one student that you share with another teacher (e.g., Title I, intervention specialist, etc.). Ask that teacher to help you brainstorm a list of questions about the student.

6. What impact does teacher action research have on the school culture?

Fluency Self-Evaluation: First Reading

Student Name: _____   Date: _____

Text: _____

Read the assigned text aloud into the tape recorder. After reading, comment on how you felt you read.

My phrasing was

○ word by word.

○ phrase by phrase.

○ partly word by word and partly phrase by phrase.

My expression was

○ was good.

○ was okay.

○ needs improvement.

I read

○ slowly.

○ just right.

○ too fast.

I immediately knew

○ some of the words.

○ most of the words.

I want to improve _____

_____

Readers Theater Parent Letter

Dear Parents,

As part of our study on what good readers sound like, students will be participating in Readers Theater. In Readers Theater, students study the lines of a script so they can become fluent with their lines. They stand in front of the class and read from their scripts. Students focus on using appropriate expression, volume, phrasing, intonation, smoothness, and pace while reading the script aloud.

Each time that students participate in Readers Theater, they will be required to bring their scripts back and forth to school so they can practice them. Students only need to practice their particular part, not the entire thing. To verify that they are practicing at home, students will need to have a parent signature sheet signed for each night. Below is a sample sheet. The sheet will be located inside your child's assignment book.

If you have any questions, please contact me at school.

Day	Parent Signature	Comments
Monday		
Tuesday		
Wednesday		
Thursday		
Friday		

Middle School Readers
Rewrite the
Fluency Scale

in Franklin Middle School,
Vallejo, California

Timothy Rasinski's Multidimensional Fluency Scale (MFS; 2004c) has four dimensions: expression/volume, phrasing, smoothness, and pace, and each dimension contains four proficiency levels (see page 107). So when Linda Ferrari-Holt read a story out loud to her seventh- and eighth-grade reluctant readers as they followed it on an overhead, she did it 16 different ways to illustrate how each category sounded!

But then the students took it to the next level and decided to "take ownership" of Rasinski! "Once they had listened to each part, we stopped and they told me in their own words what they thought each part of the rubric meant." Linda wrote down the students' descriptions and typed them up, creating a student version of the MFS (see page 107). Soon, they were using their own rubric to analyze videotapes of themselves reading poetry and plays, and the improvements were dramatic.

Believing they can improve upon the experts and obsessing on how they look to others are two qualities possessed by nearly all pre-teenagers, and these kids were no exception. Having a chance to assess themselves with their own rubric and to see themselves every week on videotape was a winning combination. Their sense of ownership of the student-friendly rubric led to an increase in their satisfaction not only with their after-school program, but also with their reading—and, in turn, their self-esteem.

Linda is a reading teacher at Benjamin Franklin Middle School in Vallejo, California, a school with a wide range of students, including many who come from low-income backgrounds. Doubling as the technology coordinator at the school, she is currently in her tenth year of teaching.

A **Close-Up** Look Into **15 Diverse Classrooms**

103

The After-School Program

Franklin's after-school program serves struggling readers recruited by their language arts teachers. It meets all year, three days each week, for one hour. Now in its third year, the voluntary program averages around 14 students per session, and includes a mix of sixth-, seventh-, and eighth-grade students who are reading an average of three years below grade level. Because their reading fluency is weak, these students tend not to do well in their other classes. Linda speculates, "Maybe they didn't get [fluency practice] when they were in elementary school."

Linda knew that in order to surmount "attitude" problems, she would have to make sure the program was fun. Since the language arts classes at the school were not using any fluency instruction at the time, she decided to structure the whole after-school program around fluency activities, using poems and Readers Theater pieces that would be practiced and performed on a regular basis. After doing repeated reading practice in small groups and pairs, students would be videotaped every week performing their pieces, and would evaluate them together, using their own rubric. Every two weeks or so, a performance was held, to which students would invite parents, family, and friends. Printed programs were created for each performance, and the performances were videotaped.

Picking appealing reading materials was a key feature of the program. Linda found two sources very successful: Roald Dahl's *Revolting Rhymes*, and Janet Allen and Patrick Daley's *Read-Aloud Anthology*, comprising 35 different stories and rhymes.

The Lesson Plan

Linda begins by reading each new selection out loud to the class, modeling fluent reading.

* While modeling, Linda explains the notion of "how you can become a character through your voice." For some students, this is a new concept.

* She starts with simple rhyming poetry. "It should be simple enough to chunk it," she advises.

* Later on, she uses short stories. She also uses Martin Luther King Jr.'s "I Have a Dream" speech, which students see on video.

* Finally, she introduces Readers Theater and the book of poems *Joyful Noise: Poems for Two Voices* (Fleischman, 2004).

* The class and the teacher read the selection chorally, in unison. "When they first read out loud," Linda says, "they were intimidated, because they were lower readers, but since they were reading it as a group, they weren't scared."

* The students and teacher go over any missed words as a whole group.

* Next, the class is split in half and each half reads alternating lines of the selection in unison.

* She asks students, "How does it sound if you read it with no punctuation? With it? Listen to it the first time and see if you need a pause here or a pause there."

The class splits into smaller groups and marks their copy of the selection for pauses. The teacher circulates to help. They then break into pairs to practice rereading the selection. The students are videotaped performing the selection.

* Before critiquing themselves, they discuss as a group what kinds of things they see in the video that the group did well.

* Students look at their video performances, using their modified fluency rubrics to evaluate their own performances, and then they discuss fluency.

* Because they have been using repeated reading, when they see themselves the first time, they think they are great readers!

* Next, they name some of the ways in which they think the group needs to improve. Finally, students fill out their own rubrics for their performances.

After two practice videotapings and accompanying discussions, the public is allowed to attend, and the public performance is also videotaped. Students can obtain a copy of their videotaped performance and a copy of the printed program. Linda records the performances in order, and they watch it from the beginning each time to see what things they are doing better both as a group and as individuals.

Evidence of Success

Linda feels that giving students the chance to evaluate their own videotaped performances is "incredibly powerful," and that it gives them a kind of timeline of their own progress. They save the programs and the DVDs of all their performances.

She got permission from the estate of Roald Dahl to write several Readers Theater pieces from his *Revolting Rhymes*. Students loved them because the rhymes were easy to read, but, she notes, some British vocabulary words needed to be taught, such as *knickers*. During the first two years, she picked the Readers Theater pieces for the class, but this year, she might give students choices, including the option of writing their own.

Linda has been looking at the scores of these students' timed oral readings, which are part of the Basic Reading Inventory (BRI) given to all students in the school. Most of the students grew in their reading levels; however, Linda noticed that lower readers improved even more than the higher ones. "The fluency practice helped them break the habit of reading words without having any clue what they mean," she explains.

Linda got positive feedback on many fronts. "I started hearing from other teachers how much their students had improved in reading aloud. They saw huge gains in self-esteem. Personally, I saw that they enjoyed reading more because they were reading better…. I had parents tell me there was a huge change in their kids."

What was obvious to teachers and parents was also obvious to the students themselves. Once they saw themselves on film, they started making huge improvements. "When you do the first one, it needs help; the second time, they can see a huge improvement; and by the third, it's done for their parent." When they started in the program, they would laugh and act silly and wouldn't stand up in the front, but by the end, they had learned to be quiet and respectful of others during the videotaping, and to do their best.

And to top it all off, their fluency rubric is now published . . . in this book!

Reflections

1. Linda's research found that the lowest readers made the most improvement through the fluency program. Speculate on why you think this might be the case.

2. This fluency instruction was implemented in an afterschool program. In what ways do you feel an afterschool program can play a key role in literacy development? Share other examples of afterschool programs that have made a difference to striving students. How do the afterschool programs you know of rate in helpful support?

3. Can you think of other examples in which kids rewrote a rubric using their own word choices? What other classroom assignments might make use of this?

4. English language learners in particular benefit a lot from illustrations and graphic support of text. How could illustrations be added to a rubric to make it more ELL-friendly?

Oral Reading Fluency Scale by the Kids
in Linda Ferrari-Holt's After-School Program

A. Expression and Volume

1. Just reads words. Reading does not sound like talking. Reads in a quiet voice.

2. Reading sometimes sounds like talking. Still has a hard time pronouncing the words. Still reads in a quiet voice.

3. Makes reading sound just like talking throughout most of the passage. Sometimes reads without expression. Voice volume is pretty good throughout the reading.

4. Reads with good expression and excitement the whole time. Varies expression and volume to show the character through your voice.

I'm going to work on _____

B. Phrasing

1. Reads words in monotone with little attention to phrasing. Reads word by word.

2. Reading sounds choppy. Stress and intonation sound wrong. Ignores punctuation.

3. Reads with run-on sentences, mid-sentence pauses for breath, and some choppiness; reasonable stress and intonation.

4. Reads with good phrasing, and some attention to expression. Pleasant to listen to.

I'm going to work on _____

C. Smoothness

1. Frequently hesitates while reading, sounds out words, and repeats words or phrases. The reader makes multiple attempts to read the same passage.

2. Reads with extended pauses or hesitations. The reader has many "rough spots."

3. Reads with occasional breaks in rhythm. The reader has difficulty with specific words and/or sentence structures.

4. Reads smoothly with some breaks, but self-corrects with difficult words and/ or sentence structures.

I'm going to work on _____

D. Pace

1. Reads slowly and laboriously.

2. Reads moderately slowly.

3. Reads fast and slow throughout reading.

4. Reads at a conversational pace throughout the reading.

I'm going to work on _____

Motivating Kids to
Read Shakespeare
in Plattsburgh, New York

When encountering complex or unfamiliar text, such as a play by Shakespeare, students benefit from a variety of approaches that will improve their ability to read expressively—to read with good prosody. If students are helped, for instance, to develop an understanding of new vocabulary and to group words into meaningful phrases for oral reading, they are likely to pronounce words more accurately and read more smoothly. In doing so, they will have a better chance of comprehending what they read and will be able to help their audience make sense of the material as well.

There are many effective methods to teach vocabulary (see, for example, Beck, McKeown & Kucan, 2002; Blachowicz & Fisher, 2005). As Fountas and Pinnell point out in a review of research on vocabulary instruction, "Reading comprehension depends on wide and rich knowledge rather than just definitional knowledge" (2006, p. 528). With this in mind, many teachers ask students to compose their own sentences using new vocabulary words in context, instead of simply copying definitions out of dictionaries. This approach, along with vocabulary aids and footnotes in textbook anthologies, can provide support for students as they attempt to read text that is very different from their everyday language.

To group words into phrases, students need to develop an ability to view punctuation marks as *cues* to the way material sounds when read. One innovative approach, "Traveling Passages" (Tibbetts, 2002), uses movement to help students pay attention to those cues, especially when studying Shakespeare or other challenging materials. A handout from a workshop at the National Council of Teachers of English (NCTE) annual convention describes the procedure:

Students read a passage while walking around the room.

When students come to a

, they change direction

. they come to a full stop

? they kneel

! they jump

: or **;** they stop and lean forward

(Tibbetts, 2002, p. 1)

Teachers who wonder how this movement would look in a classroom would benefit from a visit to Marjorie Brown's school.

Motivating Students to Read Shakespeare

We've all been there—either as students or as teachers: The designated oral reader drones on, obviously lacking any understanding of the words being spoken (and misspoken) aloud.

"It's deadly when that happens," says Marjorie Brown, an English teacher in a small community 20 miles from the Canadian border in northeastern New York. "It's painful for learners to sit in class and listen as a reader fractures the text. "But," she goes on to say, "the kids in my class are 13 or 14 years old. This is the first time they've ever tried to read Shakespeare. We can't get bogged down in the minutiae. Hearing a classmate read *enmity* as 'emity' won't make the kid into a criminal. I don't want to break up the rhythm of the reading."

Every spring for the last eight years, Marjorie has taught *Romeo and Juliet* to ninth-grade students. It's part of a yearlong survey course in the school's English curriculum. "We read *The Odyssey*, short stories, and *Romeo and Juliet*. I like to finish up the year with *The House on Mango Street* (Cisneros, 1994)—a deceivingly simple book with an authentic teenager as a female protagonist."

Oral Reading in the Classroom

"We often do oral reading in class. It's got to be safe for everyone—not just for the one who's good in English; not just for the well behaved. My classroom has to be safe. The more I say that statement, the more I realize that it guides and motivates a lot of what I do."

In Marjorie's teaching day, seventh-period ninth graders enter the room after lunch, talking to one another. They settle into their individual rectangular desks. Ms. Brown asks, "Who's in charge of Act I?" Five of the eighteen students move over to the reading area's stuffed easy chairs by the window, facing the rest of the room. Two readers, books in hand, stand in the open space, facing their classmates.

Owning a Bit of Shakespeare

Earlier, Marjorie had explained, "When we start the play, I ask small groups of students to take responsibility for each of the five acts. They get together and decide who reads what part. Giving them ownership is very important. Oh, one other thing—I ask them why we are reading Shakespeare. Here's what they often say:

Because it's in our textbook.

I hate it.

I don't know.

Because you like it, Ms. Brown.

"Then I say, 'We read it because it's important. It's about real life. Hundreds of years after it was written, we're still reading it. You are going to recognize these characters. They are going to come alive for you.'"

Back in the classroom, Marjorie asks, "So, what's happened so far in this play?" Students respond: "There's been a fight in the streets." "The streets of Verona."

Many of the members of the classroom participate in this summary, this activation of prior knowledge. It is clear that the students know that the fighting is taking place between rival houses. "They are adversaries." (*Adversary* is a vocabulary word from Act I.) There will be a vocabulary quiz tomorrow. Students have learned the words on the list by constructing their own sentences in which the words are used.

The quiz consists of a selection of these student-generated, meaning-based sentences with blanks for the vocabulary. During lunch, Marjorie had said that she doesn't treat these quizzes lightly. "Vocabulary is like money," she said. "The more you have, the richer you are."

Using Traveling Passages in Shakespeare?

Now, Marjorie is ready to show the Traveling Passages and asks the students to help her remember what needs to be done at each punctuation mark so that she can write the directions on the board. Between laughter and brief anecdotes, the students compose the list that Marjorie encountered at the workshop so long ago. They probably wish there were more exclamation marks in Shakespeare so that they could jump more frequently.

Marjorie didn't start using Traveling Passages right after going to the NCTE workshop in 2002. As many professionals do, she put the handout in a file and ran across it a few years later. "I thought, Why not try this out?" she explains.

Once she did, kids started laughing when they read Shakespeare. They also started paying attention to prosody and punctuation—finding that there's no need to pause at the end of each line as if it were the end of a sentence. They began to bump into one another as they read their parts—Shakespeare had become a "moving" experience for them.

The five students responsible for today's segment of *Romeo and Juliet* tell everyone what page they are on and then start moving in a Traveling Passages way as they read their lines aloud. This only lasts for a few minutes. They stop to say it was easier the day when they were able to have class on the auditorium stage where there was more space to move freely. Although they don't do Traveling Passages very often, Marjorie uses it as a technique to break down the barriers of Shakespeare—for, as she says, "If you want to get kids to pay attention today, you have to get them engaged."

Evidence of Success

Marjorie has found over the years that students leave her class with an ability to approach complex material with less trepidation than they had at the beginning of the year. The plays of Shakespeare become more meaningful as a result of the combination of oral practice, using vocabulary in context, active listening, and respectful discussion—classroom interactions that develop a joyful, supportive, and safe approach to learning difficult material.

"Plays are meant to be listened to," Marjorie recounts. "During class, I give the students an option of hearing the words without following along in the book." Marjorie went on to explain that this is especially important for the auditory learners. Students hear the text read aloud by individuals from the small groups who have practiced reading specific segments of the play. The small groups (and all the other students in class) are encouraged to work on a fluent oral reading of the next day's assignment as homework. As one student tells me, "It's a known fact that she wants us to read it out loud before class. I'm in my bedroom reading Shakespeare and my parents think I'm talking on the phone!"

Later, in class, after the demonstration, one of the girls in the small group reads Romeo's speech from the end of Act I, Scene 4:

> For my mind misgives
> Some consequence, yet hanging in the stars,
> Shall bitterly begin his fearful date
> With this night's revels, and expire the term
> Of a despisèd life closed in my breast
> By some vile forfeit of untimely death.
> But He that hath the steerage of my course
> Direct my sail! On, lusty gentlemen.
>   (in Deluzain et al., 1996, p. 500)

She doesn't pause at the end of each line. Perhaps she remembers that commas denote a change in direction, and periods a full stop. When the speech is done, Marjorie makes sure that everyone knows the vocabulary word *revels* means "a big party" and then facilitates a discussion about Shakespeare's use of foreshadowing—Romeo sees ahead to his own demise.

Seeing Marjorie Brown's class supports this researched-based conclusion to a T: "The most pervasive conclusion of school and teacher effectiveness studies was that teachers of reading profoundly influence how much students learn" (Blair, Rupley & Nichols, 2007, p. 436). The students in Ms. Brown's class learn that they are able to tackle something like Shakespeare.

Reflections

1. How safe do we make our classrooms for students to make mistakes?

2. When students are reading difficult text aloud, how often and in which ways should teachers intervene to assist with pronunciation? Can this be done without breaking the flow of the reading?

3. How can teachers establish a system that students can use to offer assistance to their peers during oral reading? Some teachers don't allow students to supply words until a reader says, "assist."

4. What are some ways to encourage students to discover the meaning and pronunciation of unfamiliar vocabulary (such as that often used by Shakespeare) that move beyond direct instruction and rote memorization?

5. How big a role does "ownership" play when small groups of students are responsible for presenting specific portions of literature to their peers?

6. Are there ways to involve families at our students' homes in the preparation of oral reading that will be done in the classroom?

Bibliography of Professional Literature on Fluency

List of Categories

Numbers in brackets at the end of citations refer to the following categories:

[1] Edited books on fluency

[2] Professional works that focus on several aspects of fluency

[3] Assessing fluency

[4] Comprehension and fluency

[5] Prosody: Reading with expression

[6] Prosody: Readers Theater

[7] Prosody: Singing and poetry-based approaches to fluency

[8] Prosody: Fluency and English language learners

[9] Automaticity: Reading rate

[10] Automaticity: Repeated reading

[11] Automaticity: Dyad and paired reading

[12] Accuracy: Word study and phonics

[13] Accuracy: Oral reading miscues

[14] Various approaches to promote fluency

[15] Specific programs to promote fluency

[16] General information about reading

Allington, R. L. (1983). Fluency: The neglected reading goal. *The Reading Teacher, 36*, 556–561. [2]

Allington, R. L. (2000). *What really matters for struggling readers.* New York: Allyn & Bacon. [16]

Allington, R. L. (2006). Fluency: Still waiting after all these years. In S. J. Samuels & A. E. Farstrup (Eds.), *What research has to say about fluency instruction* (pp. 94–105). Newark, DE: International Reading Association. [2]

Allington, R. L. (2008). *What really matters in fluency.* Boston: Allyn & Bacon. [2]

Allington, R. L., & McGill-Franzen, A. (2003). The impact of summer setback on the reading achievement gap. *Phi Delta Kappan, 84*, 68–75. [16]

Anderson, R. C., Wilson, P. T., & Fielding, L. G. (1988). Growth in reading and how children spend their time outside of school. *Reading Research Quarterly, 23*, 285–303. [16]

Ash, G. E., & Kuhn, M. R. (2006). Meaningful oral and silent reading in the elementary and middle school classroom: Breaking the round robin reading addiction. In T. Rasinski, C. Blachowicz, & K. Lems (Eds.), *Fluency instruction: Research-based best practices* (pp. 155–172). New York: Guilford Press. [2]

Aslett, R. (1990). *Effects of the oral recitation lesson on reading comprehension of fourth grade developmental readers.* Unpublished doctoral dissertation, Brigham Young University, Provo, UT. [4]

Baker, S. K., & Good, R. (1995). Curriculum-based measurement of English reading with bilingual Hispanic students: A validation study with second-grade students. *School Psychology Review, 24,* 561–578. [8]

Bauer, J. F., & Anderson, R. S. (2001, December/January). A constructivist stretch: Preservice teachers meet preteens in a technology-based literacy project. *Reading Online, 5*(5). Retrieved February 24, 2008, from www.readingonline.org/articles/art_index.asp?HREF=bauer/index.html. [14]

Beach, S. A. (1993). Oral reading instruction: Retiring the bird in the round. *Reading Psychology: An International Quarterly, 14,* 333–338. [14]

Bear, D. R., Invernizzi, M., Templeton, S., & Johnston, F. (2007). *Words their way: Word study for phonics, vocabulary, and spelling instruction* (4th ed.). New York: Prentice Hall. [12]

Beaver, J. (1999). *Developmental reading assessment.* New York: Scott Foresman. [13]

Beck, I. L. (2005). *Making sense of phonics: The hows and whys.* New York: Guilford. [12]

Beck, I. L., McKeown, M. G., & Kucan, L. (2002). *Bringing words to life: Robust vocabulary instruction.* New York: Guilford. [12]

Biemiller, A. (1977). Relationships between oral reading rates for letters, words, and simple text in the development of reading achievement. *Reading Research Quarterly, 13,* 223–253. [9]

Biggs, M., Homan, S., Dedrick, R., Minnick, V., & Rasinski, T. (2008). Using an interactive singing software program: A comparative study of middle school struggling readers. *Reading Psychology: An International Quarterly, 29,* 195–213. [7]

Blachowicz, C. L., & Fisher, P. (2005). *Teaching vocabulary in all classrooms* (3rd ed.). New York: Prentice Hall. [12]

Blachowicz, C. Z., Sullivan, D. M., & Cieply, C. (2001). Fluency snapshots: A quick screening tool for your classroom. *Reading Psychology, 22,* 95–109. [3]

Blair, T. R., Rupley, W. H., & Nichols, W. D. (2007). The effective teacher of reading: Considering the "what" and "how" of instruction. *The Reading Teacher, 60,* 432–438. [16]

Blum, I. H., Koskinen, P. S., Tennant, N., Parker, E. M., Straub, M., & Curry, C. (1995). Using audiotaped books to extend classroom literacy instruction into the homes of second-language learners. *Journal of Reading Behavior, 27,* 535–563. [8]

Breznitz, Z. (2007). Asynchrony: Timing differences between processing modalities can cause reading difficulties. Retrieved March 15, 2008, from www.childrenofthecode.org/interviews/breznitz.htm#RateofReading. [9]

Bromage, B. K., & Mayer, R. E. (1986). Quantitative and qualitative effects of repetition on learning from technical text. *Journal of Educational Psychology, 78,* 271–278. [10]

Carbo, M. (1978a). Teaching reading with talking books. *The Reading Teacher, 32,* 267–273. [15]

Carbo, M. (1978b). A word imprinting technique for children with severe memory disorders. *Teaching Exceptional Children, 11*(1), 3–5. [15]

Carbo, M. (1981). Making books talk to children. *The Reading Teacher, 35,* 186–189. [15]

Carbo, M. (1989). *How to record books for maximum reading gains.* Long Island, NY: National Reading Styles Institute. [15]

Carrick, L. U. (2000). *The effects of readers theatre on fluency and comprehension in fifth grade students in regular classrooms.* Unpublished doctoral dissertation, Lehigh University, Bethlehem, PA. [6]

Carrick, L. U. (2006). Readers theatre across the curriculum. In T. Rasinski, C. Blachowicz, & K. Lems (Eds.), *Fluency instruction: Research-based best practices* (pp. 209–228). New York: Guilford. [6]

Carver, R. P. (1990). *Reading rate: A review of research and theory.* San Diego: Academic Press. [9]

Carver, R. P., & Hoffman, J. V. (1981). The effect of practice through repeated reading on gain in reading ability using a computer-based instructional system. *Reading Research Quarterly, 16,* 374–390. [10]

Chall, J. S. (1996). *Stages of reading development* (2nd ed.). Fort Worth, TX: Harcourt-Brace. [16]

Chard, D. J., Vaughn, S., & Tyler, B. (2002). A synthesis of research on effective interventions for building reading fluency with elementary students with learning disabilities. *Journal of Learning Disabilities, 35,* 386–406. [2]

Chomsky, C. (1976). After decoding: What? *Language Arts, 53,* 288–296. [16]

Chow, P., & Cummins, J. (2003). Valuing multilingual and multicultural approaches to learning. In S. R. Schecter & J. Cummins (Eds.), *Multilingual education in practice: Using diversity as a resource* (pp. 32–60). Portsmouth, NH: Heinemann. [8]

Clay, M. M. (1968). A syntactic analysis of reading errors. *Journal of Verbal Learning and Verbal Behavior, 7,* 434–438. [12]

Clay, M. M. (1969). Reading errors and self correction behavior. *British Journal of Educational Psychology, 39,* 47–56. [12]

Clay, M. M. (1993). *Reading Recovery: A guidebook for teachers in training.* Portsmouth, NH: Heinemann. [15]

Clay, M. M. (2005). *Literacy lessons designed for individuals, Part One: Why? When? And How?* Portsmouth, NH: Heinemann. [16]

Clay, M. M., & Imlach, R. H. (1971). Juncture, pitch, and stress as reading behavior variables. *Journal of Verbal Learning and Verbal Behavior, 10,* 133–139. [5]

Clayton, K. (2000). Broadcast media: Enhancing literacy through video production. *Reading Online.* Retrieved November 28, 2009, from www.readingonline.org/newliteracies/lit_index. asp?HREF=action/clayton/index.ht ml. [14]

Coles, G. (2004). Danger in the classroom: "Brain glitch" research and learning to read. *Phi Delta Kappan, 85,* 344–351. [16]

Comprehension Strategies Instruction. (2009). Huntington Beach, CA: Pacific Learning. Retrieved December 1, 2009, from www.pacificlearning.com. [4]

Cunningham, P. M. (2004). *Phonics they use* (4th ed.). New York: Allyn & Bacon.

Daane, M. C., Campbell, J. R., Grigg, W. S., Goodman, M. J., & Oranje, A. (2005). *Fourth-grade students reading aloud: NAEP 2002 special study of oral reading.* Washington, DC: U.S. Department of Education, Institute of Education Sciences. [2]

D'Agostino, J. V., & Murphy, J. A. (2004). A meta-analysis of Reading Recovery in United States schools. *Educational Evaluation and Policy Analysis, 26*(1), 23–38. [15]

Dahl, P. R. (1970). An experimental program for teaching high speed word recognition and comprehension skills. In J. E. Button, T. Lovitt, & T. Rowland (Eds.), *Communications research in learning disabilities and mental retardation* (pp. 33–65). Baltimore, MD: University Park Press. [14]

Daniels, H. (1994). *Literature circles: Voice and choice in the student-centered classroom.* York, ME: Stenhouse. [16]

Deno, S. L. (1985). Curriculum-based measurement: The emerging alternative. *Exceptional Children, 52,* 219–232. [3]

Deno, S. L., Mirkin, P. K., & Chiang, B. (1982). Identifying valid measures of reading. *Exceptional Children, 49,* 36–45. [3]

Dowhower, S. L. (1987). Effects of repeated reading on second-grade transitional readers' fluency and comprehension. *Reading Research Quarterly, 22,* 389–407. [10]

Dowhower, S. L. (1991). Speaking of prosody: Fluency's unattended bedfellow. *Theory Into Practice, 30*(3), 165–175. [5]

Dowhower, S. L. (1994). Repeated reading revisited: Research into practice. *Reading and Writing Quarterly, 10,* 343–358. [10]

Duke, N. K., Pressley, M., & Hilden, K. (2004). Difficulties with reading comprehension. In C. A. Stone, E. R. Silliman, B. J. Ehren, & K. Apel (Eds.), *Handbook of language and literacy: Development and disorders* (pp. 501–520). New York: Guilford. [4]

Durkin, D. (1978). What classroom observations reveal about reading comprehension instruction. *Reading Research Quarterly, 14,* 481–533. [4]

Ehri, L. C. (2005). Learning to read words: Theory, findings, and issues. *Scientific Studies of Reading, 9,* 167–188. [16]

Eldredge, J. L. (1990). Increasing reading performance of poor readers in the third grade by using a group assisted strategy. *Journal of Educational Research, 84,* 69–77. [14]

Eldredge, J. L., & Butterfield, D. D. (1986). Alternatives to traditional reading instruction. *The Reading Teacher, 40,* 32–37. [14]

Eldredge, J. L., & Quinn, D. W. (1988). Increasing reading performance of low-achieving second graders with dyad reading groups. *Journal of Educational Research, 82,* 40–46. [11]

Eldredge, J. L., Reutzel, D. R., & Hollingsworth, P. M. (1996). Comparing the effectiveness of two oral reading practices: Round-robin reading and the shared book experience. *Journal of Literacy Research, 28,* 201–225. [14]

Fawcett, G., & Rasinski, T. (2008). Fluency strategies for struggling readers. In S. Lenski & J. Lewis (Eds.), *Reading success for struggling adolescent readers* (pp. 155–169). New York: Guilford Press. [14]

Fleischer, L. S., Jenkins, J. R., & Pany, D. (1979). Effects on poor readers' comprehension of training in rapid decoding. *Reading Research Quarterly, 15,* 30–48. [4]

Florida Center for Reading Research. (2006). *Fluency First!* [Review]. Retrieved September 5, 2006, from www.fcrr.org/FCRRReports/PDF/FluencyFirstR2.pdf. [15]

Fluency Instruction. (2007). Reading Recovery Council of North America. Retrieved October 26, 2009, from www.readingrecovery.org/reading_recovery/federal/Essential/fluency.asp. [15]

Flynt, E. S., & Cooter, R. B. (2004). *Flynt-Cooter reading inventory for the classroom* (5th ed.). Columbus, OH: Merrill. [13]

Fountas, I. C., & Pinnell, G. S. (1996). *Guided Reading: Good first teaching for all children.* Portsmouth, NH: Heinemann. [16]

Fountas, I. C., & Pinnell, G. S. (2001). *Guiding readers and writers: Teaching comprehension, genre, and content literacy.* Portsmouth, NH: Heinemann. [16]

Fountas, I. C., & Pinnell, G. S. (2006). *Teaching for comprehending and fluency: Thinking, talking and writing about reading, K–8*. Portsmouth, NH: Heinemann. [4]

Fowler, M. C., Lindemann, L. M., Thacker-Gwaltney, S., & Invernizzi, M. (2002). *A second year of one-on-one tutoring: An intervention for second graders with reading difficulties* (CIERA Rep. No. 3-019). Ann Arbor, MI: Center for the Improvement of Early Reading Achievement. [14]

Fry, E. (1998). The most common phonograms. *The Reading Teacher, 51*, 620–622. [12]

Fry, E., & Kress, J. (2006). *The reading teacher's book of lists* (5th ed.). San Francisco: Jossey-Bass. [12]

Fuchs, L. S., Fuchs, D., Hosp, M. K., & Jenkins, J. R. (2001). Oral reading fluency as an indicator of reading competence: A theoretical, empirical, and historical analysis. *Scientific Studies of Reading, 5,* 239–256. [2]

Gallagher, K. (2004). *Deeper reading: Comprehending challenging texts 4–12*. Portland, ME: Stenhouse. [16]

Gaskins, I. W., Ehri, L. C., Cress, C., O'Hara, C., & Donnelly, K. (1996–1997). Procedures for word learning: Making discoveries about words. *The Reading Teacher, 50*, 312–327. [12]

Good, R. H., III, & Kaminski, R. (2005). *DIBELS: Dynamic indicators of basic early literacy skills* (6th ed.). Eugene, OR: Institute for the Development of Educational Achievement. [3]

Good, R. H., III, Simmons, D. C., & Kame'enui, E. J. (2001). The importance and decision-making utility of a continuum of fluency-based indicators of foundational reading skills for third-grade high-stakes outcomes. *Scientific Studies of Reading, 5*, 257–288. [3]

Goodman, K. S. (1965). A linguistic study of cues and miscues in reading. *Elementary English, 42,* 639–643. [13]

Goodman, K. S. (2006). *The truth about DIBELS: What it is, what it does*. Portsmouth, NH: Heinemann. [3]

Goodman, K. S., & Burke, C. L. (1973). *Theoretically based studies of patterns of miscues in oral reading performance* (USOE Project No. 90375). Washington, DC: U.S. Department of Health, Education, and Welfare. [13]

Goodman, Y. M., & Burke, C. L. (1972). *Reading miscue inventory*. New York: MacMillan. [13]

Goodman, Y. M., & Marek, A. M. (Eds.). (1996). *Retrospective miscue analysis: Revaluing readers and reading*. Katona, NY: Richard C. Owen. [13]

Greene, F. (1979). Radio reading. In C. Pennock (Ed.), *Reading comprehension at four linguistic levels* (pp. 104–107). Newark, DE: International Reading Association. [14]

Griffith, L., & Rasinski, T. V. (2002, November). *Readers theater promotes fluency and achievement*. Paper presented at the annual meeting of the College Reading Association, Philadelphia, PA. [6]

Griffith, L. W., & Rasinski, T. V. (2004). A focus on fluency: How one teacher incorporated fluency with her reading curriculum. *The Reading Teacher, 58*, 126–137. [2]

Gunning, T. (1995). Word building: A strategic approach to the teaching of phonics. *The Reading Teacher, 48*, 484–488. [12]

Hamilton, C., & Shinn, M. R. (2000). *Characteristics of word callers: An investigation of the accuracy of teachers' judgments of reading comprehension and oral reading skills*. Eugene: University of Oregon. Retrieved June 1, 2009, from www.cbmnow.com/documents/wordcaller.pdf. [4]

Harris, T. L., & Hodges, R. E. (Eds.). (1995). *The literacy dictionary: The vocabulary of reading and writing*. Newark, DE: International Reading Association. [16]

Hasbrouck, J. E., Ihnot, C., & Rogers, G. H. (1999). "Read Naturally": A strategy to increase oral reading fluency. *Reading Research and Instruction, 39*(1), 27–38. [15]

Hasbrouck, J. E., & Tindal, G. (1992). Curriculum-based oral reading fluency norms for students in grades 2 through 5. *Teaching Exceptional Children, 24*(3), 41–44. [3]

Heckelman, R. G. (1969). A neurological impress method of reading instruction. *Academic Therapy, 4*, 277–282. [14]

Hecker, L., Burns, L., Elkind, J., Elkind, K., & Katz, L. (2002). Benefits of assistive reading software for students with attention disorders. *Annals of Dyslexia, 52*, 243–272. [15]

Henkin, R., Dipinto, V., & Hunt, J. (Eds.). (2002). Critical literacy in democratic classrooms [Themed issue]. *Democracy and Education, 14*(3). [16]

Herman, P. A. (1985). The effect of repeated readings on reading rate, speech pauses, and word recognition accuracy. *Reading Research Quarterly, 20*, 553–564. [10]

Hintze, J. M., Shapiro, E. S., & Daly, E. J., III (1998). An investigation of the effects of passage difficulty level on outcomes of oral reading fluency progress monitoring. *School Psychology Review, 27*, 433–445. [3]

Hoffman, J. V. (1987). Rethinking the role of oral reading in basal instruction. *Elementary School Journal, 87*, 367–373. [14]

Hoffman, J. V. (1991). Teacher and school effects in learning to read. In R. Barr, M. L. Kamil, P. Mosenthal, & P. D. Pearson (Eds.), *Handbook of reading research: Vol. 2* (pp. 911–950). White Plains, NY: Longman. [16]

Hoffman, J. V., & Clements, R. (1984). Reading miscues and teacher verbal feedback. *Elementary School Journal, 84*, 423–439. [13]

Hoffman, J. V., & Crone, S. (1985). The oral recitation lesson: A research-derived strategy for reading in basal texts. In J. A. Niles & R. V. Lalik (Eds.), *Issues in literacy: A research perspective* (34th yearbook of the National Reading Conference, pp. 76–83). Rockfort, NY: National Reading Conference. [14]

Hoffman, J. V., O'Neal, S., Kastler, L., Clements, R., Segel, K., & Nash, M. F. (1984). Guided oral reading and miscue focused verbal feedback in second-grade classrooms. *Reading Research Quarterly, 19*, 367–384. [13]

Hoffman, J. V., Roser, N. L., Salas, R., Patterson, E., & Pennington, J. (2001). Text leveling and "little books" in first-grade reading. *Journal of Literacy Research, 33*, 507–528. [16]

Hoffman, J. V., & Segel, K. (1983, May). *Oral reading instruction: A century of controversy (1880–1980)*. Paper presented at the annual meeting of the International Reading Association, Anaheim, CA. (ERIC Document Reproduction Service No. ED239237). [2]

Hollingsworth, P. M. (1978). An experimental approach to the impress method of teaching reading. *The Reading Teacher, 31*, 624–626. [14]

Hoskisson, K. (1975a). The many facets of assisted reading. *Elementary English, 52*, 312–315. [14]

Hoskisson, K. (1975b). Successive approximation and beginning reading. *Elementary School Journal, 75*, 442–451. [14]

Hyatt, A. V. (1943). *The place of oral reading in the school program: Its history and development from 1880–1941*. New York: Teachers College Press. [2]

Invernizzi, M., Juel, C., & Rosemary, C. A. (1997). A community volunteer tutorial that works. *The Reading Teacher, 50*, 304–311. [14]

Invernizzi, M., Rosemary, C., Juel, C., & Richards, H. C. (1997). At-risk readers and community volunteers: A three-year perspective. *Scientific Studies of Reading, 1*, 277–300. [14]

Jackson, J. B., Paratore, J. R., Chard, D. J., & Garnick, S. (1999). An early intervention supporting the literacy learning of children experiencing substantial difficulty. *Learning Disabilities: Research and Practice, 14*, 254–267. [14]

Johns, J., & Berglund, R. (2002). *Fluency: Questions, answers, evidence-based strategies.* Dubuque, IA: Kendall Hunt. [2]

Johnston, S. (2006). The fluency assessment system: Improving oral reading fluency with technology. In T. Rasinski, C. Blachowicz, & K. Lems (Eds.), *Fluency instruction: Research-based best practices* (pp. 123–140). New York: Guilford. [3]

Kame'enui, E. J., & Simmons, D. C. (2001). Introduction to this special issue: The DNA of reading fluency. *Scientific Studies of Reading, 5*, 203–210. [2]

Kame'enui, E. J., & Simmons, D. C. (Eds.). (2001). The role of fluency in reading competence, assessment, and instruction: Fluency at the intersection of accuracy and speed [Special issue]. *Scientific Studies of Reading, 5*(3). [2]

Keillor, G. (2004). *The Writer's Almanac.* [For the week of October 18, 2004.] Retrieved April 22, 2007, from writersalmanac.publicradio.org/programs/2004/10/18/index.html. [2]

Knapp, N. F., & Winsor, A. P. (1998). A reading apprenticeship for delayed primary readers. *Reading Research and Instruction, 38*, 13–29. [14]

Koskinen, P. S., & Blum, I. H. (1984). Repeated oral reading and acquisition of fluency. In J. A. Niles, & L. A. Harris (Eds.), *Changing perspectives on research in reading/language processing and instruction* (33rd yearbook of the National Reading Conference, pp. 183–187). Rochester, NY: National Reading Conference. [10]

Koskinen, P. S., & Blum, I. H. (1986). Paired repeated reading: A classroom strategy for developing fluent reading. *The Reading Teacher, 40*, 70–75. [10]

Koskinen, P. S., Blum, I. H., Bisson, S. A., Phillips, S. M., Creamer, T. S., & Baker, T. K. (1999). Shared reading, books, and audiotapes: Supporting diverse students in school and at home. *The Reading Teacher, 52*, 430–444. [8]

Koskinen, P. S., Blum, I. H., Bisson, S. A., Phillips, S. M., Creamer, T. S., & Baker, T. K. (2000). Book access, shared reading, and audio models: The effects of supporting the literacy learning of linguistically diverse students in home and school. *Journal of Educational Psychology, 92*, 23–36. [8]

Kozub, R. (2000, August). Reader's theater and its affect [sic] on oral language fluency. *Reading Online.* Retrieved November 28, 2009, from www.readingonline.org/editorial/august2000/rkrt.htm. [6]

Kuhn, M. R., Schwanenflugel, P. J., Morris, R. D., Morrow, L. M., Woo, D. G., Meisinger, E. B., Stahl, S. A. (2006). Teaching children to become fluent and automatic readers. *Journal of Literacy Research, 38*, 357–387. [2]

Kuhn, M. R., & Stahl, S. A. (2000). *Fluency: A review of developmental and remedial practices.* (CIERA Rep. No. 2-008). Ann Arbor, MI: Center for the Improvement of Early Reading Achievement, U.S. Department of Education. [2]

Kuhn, M. R., & Stahl, S. A. (2004). Fluency: A review of developmental and remedial practices. In R. B. Ruddell & N. J. Unrau (Eds.), *Theoretical models and processes of reading* (5th ed.) (pp. 412–453). Newark, DE: International Reading Association. [2]

LaBerge, D., & Samuels, S. A. (1974). Toward a theory of automatic information processing in reading. *Cognitive Psychology, 6*, 293–323. [9]

Langford, J. (2001, July). Tape assisted reading for a group of low progress readers in a secondary school. *Reading Today for Tomorrow, Auckland [NZ] Reading Association Newsletter,* 14–21. [15]

Lems, K. (2001, fall). Integrated poetry performance unit. *ELI Teaching: A Journal of Theory and Practice, 34,* 44–45. [7]

Lems, K. (2002). An American poetry project for low intermediate ESL adults. *English Teaching Forum.* Washington, DC: United States Information Agency. Available at eca.state.gov/forum/vols/vol39/no4/p24.htm. [7]

Lems, K. (2006). Reading fluency and comprehension in adult English language learners. In T. Rasinski, C. Blachowicz, & K. Lems (Eds.), *Fluency instruction: Research-based best practices* (pp. 231–252). New York: Guilford. [8]

Lems, K., Miller, L. D., & Soro, T. M. (2010). *Teaching reading to English language learners: Insights from linguistics.* New York: Guilford. [8]

Leslie, L., & Caldwell, J. (2005). *Qualitative reading inventory–4* (4ᵗʰ ed.). Boston, MA: Allyn & Bacon. [3]

Leu, D. J. (1982). Oral reading error analysis: A critical review of research and application. *Reading Research Quarterly, 17,* 420–437. [13]

Liben, D. (2008). *The unique role fluency plays in adolescent literacy programs.* Unpublished manuscript. [2]

Liben, D., & Liben, M. (2004). Our journey to reading success. *Educational Leadership, 61*(6), 58–61. [16]

Liben, D., & Liben, M. (2005). Learning to read in order to learn: Building a program for upper elementary students. *Phi Delta Kappan, 86,* 401–406. [16]

Macmillan/McGraw-Hill. (1997). *Progress assessment: Reading, writing & listening.* New York: Author. [3]

Maro, N. (2001). Reading to improve fluency. *Illinois Reading Council Journal, 29*(3), 10–18. [2]

Marston, D. B. (1989). A curriculum-based measurement approach to assessing academic performance: What it is and why do it. In M. R. Shinn (Ed.), *Curriculum-based measurement: Assessing special children* (pp. 18–78). New York: Guilford. [3]

Martinez, M., & Roser, N. (1985). Read it again: The value of repeated readings during storytime. *The Reading Teacher, 38,* 782–786. [10]

Martinez, M., Roser, N. L., & Strecker, S. (1999). "I never thought I could be a star": A readers theatre ticket to reading fluency. *The Reading Teacher, 52,* 326–334. [6]

Mathes, P. G., Torgesen, J. K., & Allor, J. H. (2001). The effects of peer-assisted literacy strategies for first-grade readers with and without additional computer-assisted instruction in phonological awareness. *American Educational Research Journal, 38,* 371–410. [12]

Mathson, D. V., Allington, R. L., & Solic, K. L. (2006). Hijacking fluency and instructionally informative assessments. In T. Rasinski, C. Blachowicz, & K. Lems (Eds.), *Fluency instruction: Research-based best practices* (pp. 106–119). New York: Guilford. [3]

Mayer, R. E. (1983). Can you repeat that? Qualitative effects of repetition and advance organizers on learning from science prose. *Journal of Educational Psychology, 75,* 40–49. [10]

McCauley, J. K., & McCauley, D. S. (1992). Using choral reading to promote language learning for ESL students. *The Reading Teacher, 45,* 526–533. [8]

McGee, L. M., & Mandel-Morrow, L. (2005). *Teaching literacy in kindergarten.* New York: Guilford. [16]

McGill-Franzen, A., & Allington, R. L. (2005). *Bridging the summer reading gap.* Retrieved October 28, 2009, from teacher.scholastic.com/products/instructor/summer_reading.htm. [16]

McGraw, L. K. (2000). Parent tutoring in repeated reading: Effects of procedural adherence on fluency, maintenance, and intervention acceptability. *Dissertation Abstracts International, 60*(7-A), 2372. [10]

McNaughton, S., Glynn, T., & Robinson, V. (1985). *Pause, prompt and praise: Effective tutoring for remedial reading.* Birmingham, United Kingdom: Positive Products. [14]

Mercer, C. D., Campbell, K. U., Miller, M. D., Mercer, K. D., & Lane, H. B. (2000). Effects of a reading fluency intervention for middle schoolers with specific learning disabilities. *Learning Disabilities: Research and Practice, 15,* 179–189. [14]

Meyer, M. S., & Felton, R. H. (1999). Repeated reading to enhance fluency: Old approaches and new directions. *Annals of Dyslexia, 49,* 283–306. [10]

Millin, S. K., & Rinehart, S. D. (1999). Some of the benefits of readers theater participation for second-grade Title I readers. *Reading Research and Instruction, 39*(1), 71–88. [6]

Moore, R. A., & Aspegren, C. M. (2001). Reflective conversations between two learners: Retrospective miscue analysis. *Journal of Adolescent & Adult Literacy, 44,* 492–503. [13]

Morgan, A., Wilcox, B. R., & Eldredge, J. L. (2000). Effect of difficulty levels on second-grade delayed readers using dyad reading. *Journal of Educational Research, 94,* 113–119. [11]

Morgan, R., & Lyon, E. (1979). Paired reading: A preliminary report on a technique for parental tuition of reading-retarded children. *Journal of Child Psychology and Psychiatry, 20,* 151–160. [11]

Morris, D. (1995). *Early Steps: An early intervention program.* Bloomington, IN: ERIC Clearinghouse on Reading, English, and Communication. (ERIC Document Reproduction Service No. ED388956). [15]

Morris, D., & Nelson, L. (1992). Supported oral reading with low achieving second graders. *Reading Research and Instruction, 32*(1), 49–63. [14]

Morris, D., Shaw, B., & Perney, J. (1990). Helping low readers in grades 2 and 3: An after-school volunteer tutoring program. *Elementary School Journal, 91,* 133–150. [14]

Morris, D., Tyner, B., & Perney, J. (2000). Early Steps: Replicating the effects of a first-grade reading intervention program. *Journal of Educational Psychology, 92,* 681–693. [15]

Moskal, M. K., & Blachowicz, C. (2006). *Partnering for fluency* (Tools for teaching literacy). New York: Guilford. [14]

Mraz, M., & Rasinski, T. V. (2007). Summer reading loss. *The Reading Teacher, 60,* 784–789. [16]

Myers, C. A. (1978). Reviewing the literature on Fernald's technique of remedial reading. *The Reading Teacher, 31,* 614–619. [14]

Nalder, S. (2002). *The effectiveness of Rainbow Reading: An audio-assisted reading program.* Huntington Beach, CA: Pacific Learning. Retrieved November 27, 2009, from www.rainbowreading.co.nz/whatis.htm#research. [15]

National Institute of Child Health and Human Development (NICHD). (2000a). *Report of the National Reading Panel. Teaching children to read: An evidence-based assessment of the scientific research literature on reading and its implications for reading instruction* (NIH Publication No. 00-4769). Washington, DC: U.S. Government Printing Office. [16]

National Institute of Child Health and Human Development (NICHD). (2000b). *Report of the National Reading Panel. Teaching children to read: Report of the subgroups* (NIH Publication No. 00-4754). Washington, DC: U.S. Government Printing Office. [16]

A Close-Up Look Into 15 Diverse Classrooms

Neill, K. (1980). Turn kids on with repeated reading. *Teaching Exceptional Children, 12*, 63–64. [10]

Ohio Literacy Alliance. (2007). *Quick and easy high school reading assessments.* Retrieved December 10, 2007, from www.ohioliteracyalliance.org/fluency/fluency.htm. [3]

Opitz, M. F., & Rasinski, T. V. (1998). *Good-bye round robin: 25 effective oral reading strategies.* Portsmouth, NH: Heinemann. [14]

O'Shea, L. J., & Sindelar, P. T. (1983). The effects of segmenting written discourse on the reading comprehension of low- and high-performance readers. *Reading Research Quarterly, 18*, 458–465. [4]

Padak, N., & Rasinski, T. V. (2005). *Fast Start for early readers: A research-based, send-home literacy program with 60 reproducible poems and activities that ensures reading success for every child.* New York: Scholastic. [15]

Paige, D. D. (2006). Increasing fluency in disabled middle school readers: Repeated reading utilizing above grade level reading passages. *Reading Horizons, 46*(3), 167–181. [10]

Pearson, P. D. (2004). *The influence of Reading Recovery on everyday classroom practice. Reading Recovery New Zealand.* Retrieved October 26, 2009, from www.readingrecovery.ac.nz/institute/downloads/davidpearson_slideshow.ppt. [15]

Perfect, K. A. (1999). Rhyme and reason: Poetry for the heart and head. *The Reading Teacher, 52*, 728–737. [7]

Pinnell, G. S., Pikulski, J. J., Wixson, K. K., Campbell, J. R., Gough, P. B., & Beatty, A. S. (1995). *Listening to children read aloud.* Washington, DC: U.S. Department of Education, Office of Educational Research and Improvement. [2]

Pluck, M. (1995a). *Rainbow Reading programme: Teachers' manual.* Nelson, New Zealand: Rainbow Reading Programme Ltd. [15]

Pluck, M. (1995b). Rainbow Reading programme: Using taped stories. *Reading Forum, 1*, 25–30. [15]

Pluck, M. (1995c). *Rainbow Reading programme: Using taped stories—The Nelson Project.* Auckland: New Zealand Reading Association. [15]

Pluck, M. (2006). "Jonathan is 11 but reading like a struggling 7-year-old": Providing assistance for struggling readers with a tape-assisted reading program. In T. V. Rasinski, C. Blachowicz, & K. Lems (Eds.), *Fluency instruction: Research-based best practices* (pp.192–208). New York: Guilford. [15]

Postlethwaite, T. N., & Ross, K. N. (1992). *Effective schools in reading: Implications for policy planners.* The Hague: International Association for the Evaluation of Educational Achievement. [16]

Prescott, J. O. (2003). The power of reader's theater. *Instructor, 112*(5), 22–26. [6]

Rainbow Reading programme. (2009). Retrieved December 1, 2009, from www.rainbowreading.co.nz. [15]

Rasinski, T. V. (1985). *A study of factors involved in reader-text interactions that contribute to fluency in reading.* Unpublished doctoral dissertation, Ohio State University, Columbus. [2]

Rasinski, T. V. (1989). Fluency for everyone: Incorporating fluency in the classroom. *The Reading Teacher, 42*, 690–693. [2]

Rasinski, T. V. (1990a). Effects of repeated reading and listening-while-reading on reading fluency. *Journal of Educational Research, 83*, 147–150. [10]

Rasinski, T. V. (1990b). Investigating measures of reading fluency. *Educational Research Quarterly, 14*(3), 37–44. [3]

Rasinski, T. V. (1990c). *The effects of cued phrase boundaries in texts.* Bloomington, IN: ERIC Clearinghouse on Reading and Communication Skills. (ERIC Document Reproduction Service No. ED313689). [2]

Rasinski, T. V. (1995). Fast Start: A parental involvement reading program for primary grade students. In W. Linek & E. Sturtevant (Eds.), *Generations of literacy* (17th yearbook of the College Reading Association, pp. 301–312). Harrisonburg, VA: College Reading Association. [15]

Rasinski, T. V. (2000). Speed does matter in reading. *The Reading Teacher, 54,* 146–151. [9]

Rasinski, T. V. (2004a). *Assessing reading fluency.* Honolulu: Pacific Resources for Education and Learning. Retrieved December 10, 2007, from www.prel.org/products/re_/assessing-fluency.htm. [3]

Rasinski, T. V. (2004b). *Creating fluent readers. Educational Leadership, 61*(6), 46–51. [2]

Rasinski, T. V. (2004c). *Multidimensional fluency scale.* Retrieved November 28, 2009, from www.ascd.org/publications/educational_leadership/mar04/vol61/num06/Creating_Fluent_Readers.aspx. [3]

Rasinski, T. V. (2006). Reading fluency instruction: Moving beyond accuracy, automaticity, and prosody. *The Reading Teacher, 59,* 704–706. [2]

Rasinski, T. V. (2007). *Teaching reading fluency artfully: A professional and personal journey.* In R. Fink & S. J. Samuels (Eds.), Inspiring reading success: Interest and motivation in an age of high-stakes testing (pp. 117–140). Newark, DE: International Reading Association. [2]

Rasinski, T. V. (Ed.) (2009). *Essential readings on fluency.* Newark, DE: International Reading Association. [1]

Rasinski, T. V. (2010). *The fluent reader: Oral reading strategies for building word recognition, fluency, and comprehension* (2nd ed.). New York: Scholastic. [2]

Rasinski, T. V., Blachowicz, C., & Lems, K. (Eds.). (2006). *Fluency instruction: Research-based best practices.* New York: Guilford. [1]

Rasinski, T. V., & Fredericks, A. D. (1991). The Akron paired reading project. *The Reading Teacher, 44,* 514–515. [11]

Rasinski, T. V., & Hoffman, J. V. (2003). Theory and research into practice: Oral reading in the school literacy curriculum. *Reading Research Quarterly, 38,* 510–522. [2]

Rasinski, T. V., & Padak, N. D. (1998). How elementary students referred for compensatory reading instruction perform on school-based measures of word recognition, fluency, and comprehension. *Reading Psychology: An International Quarterly, 19,* 185–216. [4]

Rasinski, T. V., & Padak, N. D. (2004). *Effective reading strategies: Teaching children who find reading difficult* (3rd ed.). Columbus, OH: Merrill/Prentice Hall. [16]

Rasinski, T. V., & Padak, N. D. (2005a). Fluency beyond the primary grades: Helping adolescent readers. *Voices from the Middle, 13,* 34–41. [2]

Rasinski, T. V., & Padak, N. D. (2005b). *Fluency First! Daily routines to develop reading fluency.* Columbus, OH: Wright Group/McGraw-Hill. [15]

Rasinski, T. V., & Padak, N. D. (2005c). *3-minute reading assessments: Word recognition, fluency, and comprehension: Grades 1–4.* New York: Scholastic. [3]

Rasinski, T. V., & Padak, N. D. (2005d). *3-minute reading assessments: Word recognition, fluency, and comprehension: Grades 5–8.* New York: Scholastic. [3]

Rasinski, T. V., & Padak, N. D. (2008). *From phonics to fluency: Effective teaching of decoding and reading fluency in the elementary school* (2nd ed.). New York: Addison, Wesley, Longman. [2]

Rasinski, T. V., Padak, N. D., Linek, W. L., & Sturtevant, E. (1994). Effects of fluency development on urban second-grade readers. *Journal of Educational Research, 87,* 158–165. [2]

Rasinski, T. V., Padak, N. D., McKeon, C. A., Wilfong, L. G., Friedauer, J. A., & Heim, P. (2005). Is reading fluency a key for successful high school reading? *Journal of Adolescent and Adult Literacy, 49,* 22–27. [2]

Rasinski, T. V., Rikli, A., & Johnston, S. (2009). Reading fluency: More than automaticity? More than a concern for the primary grades? *Literacy Research and Instruction, 48,* 350–361. [2]

Rasinski, T. V., & Stevenson, B. (2005). The effects of Fast Start reading, a fluency-based home involvement reading program, on the reading achievement of beginning readers. *Reading Psychology: An International Quarterly, 26,* 109–125. [15]

Rasinski, T. V., & Zimmerman, B. S. (2001). *Phonics poetry: Teaching word families.* New York: Allyn & Bacon. [7]

Rasinski, T. V., & Zutell, J. B. (1996). Is fluency yet a goal of the reading curriculum? In E. G. Sturtevant & W. M. Linek (Eds.), *Growing literacy* (18th yearbook of the College Reading Association, pp. 237–246). Harrisonburg, VA: College Reading Association. [2]

Reitsma, P. (1988). Reading practice for beginners: Effects of guided reading, reading-while-listening, and independent reading with computer-based speech. *Reading Research Quarterly, 23,* 219–235. [14]

Renaissance Learning. (2006). *STAR Reading.* Wisconsin Rapids, WI: Author. Retrieved Nov. 29, 2009, from www.renlearn.com/starreading/overview/default.htm. [15]

Reutzel, D. R. (2006). "Hey, teacher, when you say 'fluency,' what do you mean?": Developing fluency in elementary classrooms. In T. V. Rasinski, C. Blachowicz, & K. Lems (Eds.), *Fluency instruction: Research-based best practices* (pp. 62–85). New York: Guilford. [2]

Reutzel, D. R., & Hollingsworth, P. M. (1993). Effects of fluency training on second graders' reading comprehension. *Journal of Educational Research, 86,* 325–331. [4]

Reutzel, D. R., Hollingsworth, P. M., & Eldredge, J. L. (1994). Oral reading instruction: The impact on student reading development. *Reading Research Quarterly, 29,* 40–62. [2]

Rinehart, S. D. (1999). "Don't think for a minute that I'm getting up there": Opportunities for readers' theater in a tutorial for children with reading problems. *Reading Psychology: An International Quarterly, 20*(1), 71–89. [6]

Rose, M. (2004). *Week-by-week homework for building reading comprehension and fluency: Grades 3–6.* New York: Scholastic. [4]

Rosenblatt, L. (1978). *The reader, the text, and the poem: The transactional theory of literary work.* Carbondale: Southern Illinois University Press. [16]

Samuels, S. J. (1979). The method of repeated readings. *The Reading Teacher, 32,* 403–408. [10]

Samuels, S. J. (2002). Reading fluency: Its development and assessment. In A. Farstrup & S. J. Samuels (Eds.), *What research has to say about reading instruction* (3rd ed., pp. 166–183). Newark, DE: International Reading Association. [2]

Samuels, S. J. (2007). The DIBELS tests: Is speed of barking at print what we mean by reading fluency? *Reading Research Quarterly, 42,* 563–566. [3]

Samuels, S. J., & Farstrup, A. E. (Eds.). (2006). *What research has to say about fluency instruction.* Newark, DE: International Reading Association. [1]

Santa, C. M., & Hoien, T. (1999). An assessment of Early Steps: A program for early intervention of reading problems. *Reading Research Quarterly, 34,* 54–79. [15]

Scholastic. (1999). *Scholastic Reading Inventory using the Lexile Framework technical manual, forms A and B.* Retrieved May 25, 2009, from teacher.scholastic.com/products/sri/overview/lexiles.htm. [3]

Schreiber, P. A. (1980). On the acquisition of reading fluency. *Journal of Reading Behavior, 12,* 177–186. [2]

Schreiber, P. A. (1987). Prosody and structure in children's syntactic processing. In R. Horowitz & S. J. Samuels (Eds.), *Comprehending oral and written language* (pp. 243–270). New York: Academic Press. [5]

Schreiber, P. A. (1991). Understanding prosody's role in reading acquisition. *Theory Into Practice, 30*(3), 158–164. [5]

Schreiber, P. A., & Read, C. (1980). Children's use of phonetic cues in spelling, parsing, and—maybe—reading. *Bulletin of the Orton Society, 30,* 209–224. [5]

Searfoss, L. (1975). Radio Reading. *The Reading Teacher, 29,* 295–296. [14]

Semonick, M. A. (2001). The effects of paired repeated reading on second graders' oral reading and on-task behavior. *Dissertation Abstracts International, 62*(3-1A), 914. [10]

Sibberson, F., & Szymusiak, K. (2003). *Still learning to read: Teaching students in grades 3–6.* Portland, ME: Stenhouse. [14]

Sindelar, P. T., Monda, L. E., & O'Shea, L. J. (1990). Effects of repeated readings on instructional- and mastery-level readers. *Journal of Educational Research, 83,* 220–226. [10]

Smith, F. (2006). *Reading without nonsense* (4th ed.). New York: Teachers College Press. [16]

Smith, J., & Elley, W. (1997). *How children learn to read: Insights from the New Zealand experience.* Katonah, NY: Richard C. Owen. [16]

Snow, C. E., Burns, M. S., & Griffin, P. (Eds.). (1998). *Preventing reading difficulties in young children.* Washington, DC: National Academies Press. [16]

Stahl, S. A. (1992). Saying the "p" word: Nine guidelines for exemplary phonics instruction. *The Reading Teacher, 45,* 618–625. [12]

Stahl, S. A. (2004). What do we know about fluency? Findings of the National Reading Panel. In P. McCardle & V. Chhabra (Eds.), *The voice of evidence in reading research* (pp. 187–211). Baltimore, MD: Brookes. [2]

Stahl, S. A., & Heubach, K. (2005). Fluency-oriented reading instruction. *Journal of Literacy Research, 37*(1), 25–60. [2]

Stahl, S. A., Heubach, K., & Cramond, B. (1997). *Fluency-oriented reading instruction* (Reading Research Rep. No. 79). Athens, GA, and College Park, MD: National Reading Research Center. [2]

Stahl, S. A., & Kuhn, M. R. (2002). Making it sound like language: Developing fluency. *The Reading Teacher, 55,* 582–584. [2]

Stallings, J. (1980). Allocated academic learning time revisited, or beyond time on task. *Educational Researcher, 9,* 11–16. [14]

Stanovich, K. E. (1980). Toward an interactive-compensatory model of individual differences in the development of reading fluency. *Reading Research Quarterly, 16,* 32–71. [2]

Stevenson, B. (2002). *Efficacy of the Fast Start parent tutoring program in the development of reading skills of first grade students.* Unpublished doctoral dissertation, Ohio State University, Columbus. [15]

Strecker, S., Roser, N., & Martinez, N. (1998). Toward an understanding of oral reading fluency. In T. Shanahan & F. Rodriguez-Brown (Eds.), *47th yearbook of the National Reading Conference* (pp. 295–310). Chicago: National Reading Conference. [2]

Bibliography of Professional Literature on Fluency

Sweeney, A. (2004a). *Fluency lessons for the overhead: Grades 2–3*. New York: Scholastic. [14]

Sweeney, A. (2004b). *Fluency lessons for the overhead: Grades 4–6*. New York: Scholastic. [14]

Taguchi, E. (1997). The effects of repeated readings on the development of lower identification skills of FL readers. *Reading in a Foreign Language, 11*, 97–119. [8]

Taguchi, E., & Gorsuch, G. J. (2002). Transfer effects on repeated EFL reading on reading new passages: A preliminary investigation. *Reading in a Foreign Language, 14*, 43–45. [8]

Tompkins, G. E. (2006). *Literacy for the 21st century: A balanced approach* (4th ed.). Columbus, OH: Merrill Prentice Hall. [16]

Topping, K. (1987a). Paired reading: A powerful technique for parent use. *The Reading Teacher, 40*, 608–614. [11]

Topping, K. (1987b). Peer tutored paired reading: Outcome data from ten projects. *Educational Psychology, 7*, 133–145. [11]

Topping, K. (1989). Peer tutoring and paired reading: Combining two powerful techniques. *The Reading Teacher, 42*, 488–494. [11]

Topping, K. (1995). *Paired reading, spelling and writing*. New York: Cassell. [11]

Trabasso, T., & Suh, S. (1993). Understanding text: Achieving explanatory coherence through on-line inferences and mental operations in working memory. *Discourse Processes, 16*(1/2), 3–34. [16]

Turpie, J., & Paratore, J. (1995). Using repeated reading to promote reading success in a heterogeneously grouped first grade. In K. A. Hinchman, D. J. Leu, & C. K. Kinzer (Eds.), *Perspectives on literacy research and practice* (44th yearbook of the National Reading Conference, pp. 255–263). Chicago: National Reading Conference. [10]

Tyler, B. J., & Chard, D. (2000). Using readers theater to foster fluency in struggling readers: A twist on the repeated reading strategy. *Reading and Writing Quarterly, 16*, 163–168. [6]

Vacca, J. L., Vacca, R. T., & Gove, M. K. (2000). *Reading and learning to read*. New York: Allyn & Bacon. [16]

Walker, B. J. (2003). The cultivation of student self-efficacy in reading and writing. *Reading and Writing Quarterly, 19*, 173–187. [16]

Walker, B. J., Mokhtari, K., & Sargent, S. (2006). Reading fluency: More than fast and accurate reading. In T. V. Rasinski, C. Blachowicz, & K. Lems (Eds.), *Fluency instruction: Research-based best practices* (pp. 86–105). New York: Guilford. [2]

Wheldall, K. (2000). Does Rainbow repeated reading add value to an intensive literacy intervention program for low-progress readers? An experimental evaluation. *Educational Review, 52*(1), 29–36. [15]

Wilkinson, I., Wardrop, J. L., & Anderson, R. C. (1988). Silent reading reconsidered: Reinterpreting reading instruction and its effects. *American Educational Research Journal, 25*, 127–144. [16]

Willingham, D. (2006–2007). The usefulness of brief instruction in reading comprehension strategies. *American Educator, 30*(4), 39–50. [4]

Worthy, J. (2005). *Readers theater for building fluency: Strategies and scripts for making the most of this highly effective, motivating, and research-based approach to oral reading*. New York: Scholastic. [6]

Worthy, J., & Broaddus, K. (2002). Fluency beyond the primary grades: From group performance to silent, independent reading. *The Reading Teacher, 55*, 334–343. [2]

Worthy, J., & Prater, K. (2002). "I thought about it all night": Readers theatre for reading fluency and motivation. *The Reading Teacher, 56,* 294–297. [6]

Wright Group. (1996). *SUNSHINE assessment guide: Grades K–1.* Bothell, WA: Author. [3]

Zeigler, L. L., & Johns, J. L. (2005). *Visualization: Using mental images to strengthen comprehension.* Dubuque, IA: Kendall/Hunt. [16]

Zutell, J., Donelson, R., Bevans, J., & Todt, P. (2006). Building a focus on oral reading fluency into individual instruction for struggling readers. In T. V. Rasinski, C. Blachowicz, & K. Lems (Eds.), *Fluency instruction: Research-based best practices* (pp. 265–278). New York: Guilford. [2]

Zutell, J., & Rasinski, T. V. (1991). Training teachers to attend to their students' oral reading fluency. *Theory Into Practice, 30,* 211–217. [2]

References for Other Works Mentioned

Ackland, R. T. (1999). Looking into complexity: Revisiting and revising during classroom research. *Language Arts, 77,* 40–43.

Bandura, A. (1982). Self-efficacy mechanism in human agency. *American Psychologist, 31,* 122–147.

Bandura, A. (1989). Social cognitive theory. In R. Vasta (Ed.), *Annals of child development. Vol. 6: Six theories of child development* (pp. 1-60). Greenwich, CT: JAI Press.

Bloom, B., & Biet, P. (1999). *Wolf.* New York: Orchard Books.

Cengage Learning. (2010). General OneFile. Retrieved September 3, 2010 from http://www.gale.cengage.com/PeriodicalSolutions/generalOnefile.htm?grid=GeneralOneFileRedirect

Christensen, L. (1994). Building community from chaos. In W. Au, B. Bigelow, & S. Karp (Eds.), *Rethinking our classrooms* (pp. 50–55). Milwaukee, WI: Rethinking Schools.

Cisneros, S. (1994). *The house on Mango Street.* New York: Knopf.

Crichton, M. (2008). *Prey.* New York: Avon Books.

Deluzain, H. E., et al. (Eds.). (1996). *Adventures in reading.* Austin, TX: Holt, Rinehart and Winston.

Dr. Seuss [Geisel, T. S.], & Prelutsky, J. (1998). *Hooray for Diffendoofer Day!* New York: Alfred A. Knopf.

Fleischman, P. (2004). *Joyful noise: Poems for two voices.* New York: HarperCollins.

Gorman, C. (1999). *Dork in disguise.* New York: HarperCollins.

Kidd, S. M. (2003). *The secret life of bees.* Toronto, ON: Penguin Books.

Korenblit, M. (2001). *Until we meet again: A true story of love and survival in the Holocaust.* Naugatuck, CT: Miracle Press.

Lowry, L. (1989). *Number the stars.* New York: Houghton-Mifflin.

Mayer, M. (1969). *Frog, where are you?* New York: Dial Books.

Mitchell, M. (1936). *Gone with the wind.* London, UK: Macmillan.

Mora, P. (1997). *Tomás and the library lady.* New York: Alfred Knopf.

New Heights Reading Series. (2009). Retrieved December 1, 2009, from www.brightpointliteracy.com/browse/New-Heights/24/.

Pajares, F., & Schunk, D. (2002). Self-beliefs in psychology and education: An historical perspective. In J. Aronson (Ed.), *Improving academic achievement* (pp. 3–21). New York: Academic Press.

Paterson, K. (1977). *The bridge to Terabithia.* New York: HarperCollins.

Poe, E. A. (2004). The tell-tale heart: A retelling of the short story. In J. Allen & P. Daley (Eds.), *Read-aloud anthology* (pp. 45–46). New York: Scholastic Teaching Resources.

Poetry Alive! (2007). *Resources for educators.* Retrieved December 15, 2007, from www.poetryalive.com.

Polacco, P. (1994). *My rotten redheaded older brother.* New York: Simon & Schuster.

Pool, B., Parkin, C., & Parkin, C. (2000). *PROBE: Tester's guide and answers.* Whangarei, New Zealand: Triune.

Rowling, J. K. (2007). *Harry Potter and the deathly hallows.* New York: Scholastic.

Sachar, L. (1998). *Holes.* New York: Farrar, Straus & Giroux.

Scieszka, J. (1995). *The math curse.* New York: Viking.

Sebold, A. (2007). *The lovely bones.* Boston, MA: Back Bay Books.

Shepherd, A. (2009). *Readers theater editions.* Retrieved November 28, 2009, from aaronshep.com/rt/RTE.html.

Speak out readers' theater (2009). Huntington Beach, CA: Pacific Learning. Retrieved December 1, 2009, from www.pacificlearning.com.

Tibbetts, T. (2002). *Your imaginary forces work: Teaching Shakespeare with performance.* Presentation at the meeting of the National Council of Teachers of English, Atlanta, Georgia.

Tibbetts, T. (2009). *Mainely Shakespeare: A website dedicated to the teaching of Shakespeare through the performing arts.* Retrieved December 6, 2009, from mainelyshakespeare.com.

Time for Kids. (2007). Retrieved November 28, 2009, from www.timeforkids.com/

Tuckman, B. W. (1999, August). *A tripartite model of motivation for achievement: Attitude/Drive/ Strategy.* Paper presented in the Symposium: Motivational Factors Affecting Student Achievement— Current Perspectives. Annual Meeting of the American Psychological Association, Boston.

Weekly Reader. (2007). Weekly Reader Corporation. Retrieved November 28, 2009, from weeklyreader.com.

Woolfolk, A. (2004). *Educational psychology* (9th ed.). Boston, MA: Pearson.